"Knowing how to invest is no longer a luxury in ... a necessity for all working Americans who hop... years. Julie Jason has cleverly brought to life th......... process."
— J. Carter Beese, Jr., Vice Chairman, Alex. Brown International and former Commissioner of the SEC

"This book is excellent reading. It is one of the best compilations of every aspect of 401(k)s. It is what the plan participant needs to know!"
— Michael S. Caccesse, Senior Vice President, General Counsel & Secretary, Association for Investment Management and Research

"Whether you're investing in a 401(k) plan for the first time or looking for ways to make your existing retirement investments work harder, *You and Your 401(k)* offers clear, complete, and essential advice. Required reading for people who want their post-retirement years to be comfortable ones."
— Catherine Cavender, Executive Editor, *McCall's*

"This is the most complete and in-depth book about 401(k) plans. The many examples and worksheets throughout the book will help investors to make confident and sound decisions regarding their 401(k) participation and asset allocation to maximize the chances for a successful retirement."
— Carl G. Gargula, JD, Managing Director and General Counsel, Ibbotson Associates

"An extremely valuable resource for people like me who are benefits practitioners, as well as for participants and would-be participants."
— Norwood Morrison, Benefits Manager, Framatome Technologies

"*You and Your 401(k)* provides the reader with a very thorough yet concise and easy-to-understand overview of 401(k)s. This book is not boring and is guaranteed to make you think. I feel comfortable recommending Julie Jason's book to new 401(k) participants and administrators as well as seasoned veterans in the retirement planning field."
— R. Bruce Musselman, Benefits Manager, Hatfield Quality Meats, Inc.

"Very thorough. For someone with a basic knowledge level of their 401(k) plan, this book can take them to the next level of being a more sophisticated retirement investor and planner."
— Paul Yakoboski, Research Associate, Employee Benefits Research Institute

YOU AND YOUR

401(k)

How to Manage Your 401(k)
for Maximum Returns

JULIE JASON

A FIRESIDE BOOK
Published by Simon & Schuster

FIRESIDE
Rockefeller Center
1230 Avenue of the Americas
New York, NY 10020

FIRESIDE and colophon are registered trademarks
of Simon & Schuster Inc.

Designed by Irving Perkins Associates

Manufactured in the United States of America

1 3 5 7 9 10 8 6 4 2

Library of Congress Cataloging-in-Publication Data

Jason, Julie.
You and your 401(k) : how to manage your 401(k) for maximum
returns / Julie Jason.
p.   cm.
"Fireside book."
Includes index.
(alk. paper)
1. 401 (k) plans.   I. Title.
HD7105.45.U6J25   1996
332.024′01 — dc20   96-12552
                                                              CIP

ISBN 0-684-81401-3

In view of the complex, individual, and specific nature of financial matters, this book is not intended to replace professional, individual advice. This publication contains the opinions and ideas of its author. It is sold with the understanding that the author and publisher are not engaged in rendering legal, accounting, or other professional services. Laws vary from state to state, and if the reader requires expert assistance or legal advice, a competent professional should be consulted.

The author and publisher specifically disclaim any responsibility for any liability, loss, or risk, personal or otherwise, which is incurred as a consequence, directly or indirectly, of the use of any of the ideas in this book.

To my daughters,
Ilona and Leila,
who taught me to listen,
to my mother, whose patience inspired me,
to my father, who taught me to keep things simple,
and to HGB, my friend and mentor,
who taught me to accept the uncertainty of the markets.

Contents

----

8 Contents

Acknowledgments

The tax and operational aspects of 401(k)s are highly technical and require specialized working knowledge of the current tax and labor laws as well as their practical applications. Pension and tax experts provided assistance in assuring the accuracy of the technical information provided in this book.

Special thanks are due Manuel A. Bernardo, Esq., Director of the Employee Benefits Tax Practice for the Connecticut offices of Deloitte & Touche, LLP (Stamford, Connecticut). Mr. Bernardo has been of immeasurable assistance from the early stages of the project. His knowledge of the regulatory environment, his practical approach, and his quick responsiveness proved invaluable in the face of time pressures in the preparation of the manuscript.

Mr. Bernardo's expertise comes from more than 20 years of practice in the pension field. Corporations and nonprofit organizations retain Mr. Bernardo for counsel on all aspects of the structure and operation of 401(k)s, as well as the tax, operations, and planning aspects of different types of employee benefits plans and executive compensation programs.

Catherine S. Bardsley, Esq., provided input to the special issues and rights chapters. Ms. Bardsley is counsel to the law firm of Kirkpatrick & Lockhart LLP in Washington, D.C., where she advises plan sponsors on the design and operation of various types of retirement plan programs, including 401(k) plans. Daniel L. Daniels, Esq., of Cummings & Lockwood of Stamford, Connecticut, provided trusts and estates insights.

Friends, notably Clifford J. Alexander, Esq., of the law firm of Kirkpatrick & Lockhart; Virginia A. Dwyer, former Treasurer of AT&T Corporation; Dorothy F. Haughey, Corporate Secretary of PaineWebber, Inc.; Ishier Jacobson, former President and CEO of Citizens Utilities Company; and Gayle B. Wilhelm, Esq., of the law firm of Cummings & Lockwood, opened doors to valuable resources.

The following individuals brought depth to the book by discussing their views on investor education, sharing information about how their plans operated or offering samples of their plan literature: Anthony D'Andrea, CEBS, AT&T Corporation Group Manager, Defined Contribution Plans; Lawrence S. Caruso, VP — Compensation and Benefits, General Re Corporation; Edward R. Conrad, Business Consultant, E.I. du Pont de Nemours and Company; Dolores J. Ennico, Director of Employee Services, Olin Corporation, Chemicals Division; Jo Ann Farrall, Manager — Corporate Benefits, Citizens Utilities Company; Raymond A. Gaydos, Manager, Profit Sharing, Marriott International, Inc.; James A. Heller, VP and Managing Director — Savings Plans and Other Post-Employment Benefits, AT&T Investment Management Corporation; David Hom, Executive Director, Corporate Benefits, Pitney Bowes, Inc.; John H. Korenko, Financial Manager, Human Resources, E.I. du Pont de Nemours and Company; Michael E. McClure, Director of Risk Management, Navios Corporation; Patricia M. Nazemetz, Director of Benefits, Xerox Corporation; Merrilyn Payne, Director of Human Resources, Silver Hill Hospital; Joyce Phillips, Director — Head of Human Resources, Barclays Bank — BZW; and Paul A. Rivera, Director of Benefits Planning and Design, American Brands, Inc.

Of the 401(k) participants who offered questions and concerns, special thanks are due to Charlie Conrad, Jayne Ferguson, Charlie Ponger, Anne Principe, Esq., Jane Salmonsen, and Shelly Stuart.

Finally, thanks to author Clifford R. Ennico, Esq., of the Hartford, Connecticut, law firm of Pepe & Hazard, for his thoughts on writing and his encouragement in the project; JoAnn Dohanich, Keri McDermott, Holly Cliggott, and Susan McKittrick for their input on the manuscript; Julie Castiglia of Del Mar, California, my agent, for grace, speed, and effectiveness; and to the finest editor a writer could ever hope for, Rebecca T. Cabaza, who made this project so fulfilling that I am compelled to write again.

Introduction

This book will help you make the decisions that could very possibly provide you *substantial* after-tax income in retirement. In optimal cases, depending on your age, the investment choices you make, matching funds paid by your company, and your withdrawal strategy, you may well make more in yearly after-tax retirement income from your 401(k) than you do in salary before you retire.

If you work for a small, medium, or large corporation, in all likelihood, your company offers a 401(k) or is considering offering one for its employees. A 401(k) is a tax-advantaged savings plan available only through your employer. (A similar type of plan called a 403(b) is offered to employees of nonprofit organizations.) Most of these plans are self-directed, meaning you, the employee, decide what to do with your savings.

The 401(k) is rapidly growing in popularity, with more than 25 million participants. As a professional investment adviser, I receive more and more requests from my clients for advice on where they should put their 401(k) money and why. This book will guide you in that regard and will help you maximize your plan so that you don't inadvertently pass up compounding opportunities, overestimate the budgetary effect of salary reductions, or underestimate the remarkable potential of the 401(k).

The 401(k) is the single most powerful and efficient means of (1) creating substantial retirement capital and (2) converting that capital into a substantial after-tax retirement income stream. In comparing alternatives, there is no other investment vehicle that can even begin to compete with the 401(k) in terms of the potential for building retirement assets and creating retirement income, particularly if your company contributes to your plan.

In this book, I'll introduce you to the 401(k)'s six design features — I call them "compounding elements" — that promote the potential for growth. By compounding I mean the multiplier effect. Four of these compounding elements offer immediate compounding without exposure to market risk, credit risk, leverage, or any other portfolio enhancement techniques. I will help you identify the optimal leverage points offered by the compounding elements of your particular plan and show you how to put them to work for you.

In addition, in order to help you invest your 401(k) appropriately, I will identify three 401(k) phases, each of which is governed by a different set of investment objectives. You'll learn how to manage your 401(k) investment decisions as you move through the three phases of your 401(k).

Keep in mind that all 401(k) investment activity has only two primary purposes: (1) to grow your capital — so that it can (2) produce an adequate income stream for you in retirement. All 401(k) participants need to educate themselves about the effective use of their 401(k) investment selections to achieve these purposes.

An undue fear of losing money over the short term is the single most harmful element of 401(k) investing. First, risk is inherent in every investment and needs to be managed, not avoided. Second, risk has broader meaning than just loss of principal. Most notably, the risk of loss of purchasing power is equally important to consider in a 401(k), because of the long-term nature of the investment enterprise. This book provides a methodology for investment selection that embraces risk instead of avoiding it.

Finally, it is difficult to assess the value of your 401(k) without understanding how to get your money out of your plan. I'll show you ways to withdraw from your plan so that you can pay yourself satisfactory after-tax "pension" checks during your retirement. This book is *not* meant to provide you with definitive tax guidance. Please be certain to review all the tax aspects of your participation with your accountant or tax attorney, particularly the tax effect of different withdrawal strategies.

Without a frame of reference, it is difficult to put into perspective the repercussions of the participation, contribution, investment, borrowing, and withdrawal decisions you will be called upon to make in your plan. As you read this book and follow the illustrations, you will begin to see the consequences of various 401(k) decisions. As you build on your knowledge, all the decisions you are called upon to make in your 401(k) will fall into place.

The first part of this book provides the basic background information that will show you how to think of your 401(k). Later chapters take you through the decisions you will be making as a participant. Understanding the consequences of your actions — or inaction — will help you avoid the most common mistakes 401(k) participants make with their plans.

In addition to avoiding mistakes, I will teach you how to recognize the leverage points in your plan, so that you can take full advantage of the benefits your plan offers you. These are important chapters to read, since you will begin to see how the very simplest of decisions can greatly affect your results. At the end of these chapters you will find a list of questions about your plan that you need to have answered to enable you to weigh your options.

Then, I will point out special situations such as death, disability, financial hardship, loans, and considerations for the highly compensated. Finally, I'll explain your rights and responsibilities as a 401(k) participant and discuss where to go from here.

The process I will take you through will help you take an active role in making your retirement secure and satisfying, using your 401(k) as the backbone of your retirement fund. Many of you who read this book and take charge of your 401(k) will not have to rely solely on your company pension or Social Security to provide for you in retirement. You will be able you rely on yourself and your 401(k).

1

Using Your 401(k) to
Secure Your Future

Think of your 401(k) as a valuable investment tool that can create
an extra income stream for you in retirement. Used correctly, your
401(k) can help you fill the gap between what you will need in
retirement and what you will get from your pension and Social
Security.

Moreover, in optimal cases, you may be able to pay yourself
monthly checks from your 401(k) that are actually larger than
your preretirement paychecks, even after you account for income
taxes. In addition, with appropriate tax and investment planning
continuing into retirement, your checks could cover living expenses as they rise due to the effect of inflation.

The features common to most 401(k)s translate into potential
for growth — more potential than is offered by any other type of
taxable savings or investment program. 401(k)s offer:

■ **Immediate tax advantages.** All of your earnings are subject to
tax — except the amount you tell your employer to set aside to
fund your 401(k). The amounts set aside in your 401(k)'s
pretax account are not included in your W-2 for current
income tax purposes. The benefit to you is twofold. First, you
are getting a tax break, that is, your income taxes will be lower
after you enroll. (You can approximate your annual tax savings by multiplying your effective tax rate by the amount you

17

set aside in your 401(k) during the year. Your effective tax rate is the ratio of your taxes to your income. If you look at last year's tax return and divide your taxes by your gross income, you can compute your effective tax rate. To keep things simple, I will use 25 percent as the effective tax rate in the examples in this book, unless otherwise indicated. Your rate will be higher or lower, depending on your earnings, exemptions, and deductions.) Second, because you are investing income you earned that was not reduced by taxes, you are ahead of any other investor or possible alternative investment or savings account you might be considering.

- **Continuing tax advantages.** When you invest on your own through a broker or mutual fund, or save at a bank, each year, you receive a statement (Form 1099) showing you the interest, dividends, or capital gains subject to income or capital gains taxes. Each year, you need to report these amounts on your income tax return and pay appropriate federal and state taxes. Because of the preferential treatment of 401(k)s under the tax laws, you will not get a yearly 1099 for your 401(k), and you will not have to report to the IRS any dividends, interest, or capital gains earned in your 401(k) until you withdraw money from your 401(k), which is normally at retirement. Not paying current taxes on the growth of your 401(k) creates an environment in which there is the possibility for faster "compounding" than is available in a regular, non–tax-deferred account. Faster compounding is achieved when earnings are reinvested without reduction for income taxes. I will discuss the concept of compounding more fully in Chapter 2.

- **A special bonus for participating in your 401(k).** Many employers will pay a special "bonus" into your 401(k) just for your participating. As with the employee's contribution, the employer's contribution is not currently taxed. If you have a plan that provides company matching or a profit-sharing contribution from your employer, you have a 401(k) with the most growth potential of all.

In addition to the potential for greater growth rates, there are other features of 401(k)s from which you might benefit.

- **Your company provides you prescreened investment options to choose from.** Your plan offers a selection of investment options that have been chosen for you by your employer. If you were investing on your own, you would need to spend a great deal of time and energy screening appropriate investment vehicles for your portfolio, since the universe of alternatives would be available to you. With a prescreened list of possible choices, your job as an investor becomes much less daunting and results should be much more manageable.
- **Payroll deductions are a painless way to save.** Possibly the most difficult part of saving or investing is finding money to set aside regularly. The demands of a consumer-based society are many and personal horizons are short-term. With a 401(k) your employer makes it easy for you to save for your future. Since your employer deducts 401(k) contributions from your paycheck, you can pay yourself first, painlessly.

I will be coming back to these features throughout this book in order to help you fully understand them and appreciate their significance. First, I will discuss the nature of the 401(k) and give you some insight into how to think of your plan and how you might benefit from it.

What exactly is a 401(k)? The 401(k) and its sister 403(b) are sections of the Internal Revenue Code dealing with benefit plans offered by employers to their employees. Under these sections, employers may offer savings plans for eligible employees in before-tax and after-tax dollars, with tax-deferral benefits, company matches, profit sharing, loan provisions, and a number of different investment options for the employee to choose from. The 401(k) is offered to individuals employed by small, medium, and large companies.

The 403(b) is offered to individuals employed by nonprofit, tax-exempt organizations such as hospitals, colleges and other schools, charities, and religious organizations. Both types of plans are generally available to full-time employees over the age of 21 who have been employed for a year or more.

Some companies call their 401(k)s by other names, such as a company "savings" plan. If you are not certain whether your company offers a 401(k) or if you are eligible, check with your personnel director, human resources department, or benefits department.

Unlike the traditional pension plan, the 401(k) gives you the power to control your retirement income. In a traditional defined-benefit pension plan, your employer funds your pension. At retirement, your pension pays you a monthly check, the amount of which is usually a percentage of your earnings. Most corporate pensions do not have cost of living adjustments. As a result, your monthly pension check would be the same fixed dollar amount throughout your retirement, with no increases to cover rises in the cost of living due to inflation.

Until relatively recently, the impact of inflation on pension payments was less of a concern. What has changed is longevity. People live longer. It is not unusual to see individuals needing to support themselves in retirement for twenty or thirty years or more.

Leaving aside the double-digit inflationary period of the 1970s and 1980s, historically, over long periods of time, annual inflation has averaged 3 percent. This rate of inflation might be relatively insignificant for someone who retires at age 65 and lives to age 72. On the other hand, at a 3 percent inflation rate, someone who is on a fixed dollar pension that just covers current expenses at age 65 will find that only one-half his costs are covered at age 89.

At a 3 percent inflation rate, someone age 89 can expect to need two dollars for every dollar he spent on living expenses at the age of 65. For example, if you need $40,000 to cover your living expenses when you are 65, you will require $80,000 at the age of 89 to pay for the same goods and services you paid $40,000 for when you were 65.

Looking at it another way, at 3 percent inflation, $40,000 at the age of 65 has the buying power of only $20,000 at the age of 89. That is, at 3 percent inflation, over a 24-year period, the buying power of money falls by 50 percent.

If you want a quick rule of thumb for computing the effect of inflation — or for that matter, the effect of compounding — use the rule of 72. For example, to determine how many years it will take for a number to double at a 3 percent rate, divide 72 by 3: 72 divided by 3 = 24. What this means is that at a 3 percent rate, every 24 years, doubling takes place by the operation of mathematics.

During the high inflationary 20-year period ending in 1993, the rate of inflation averaged 6 percent. Using the rule of 72, you can see that at 6 percent, doubling (or halving) occurs every 12 years. This means that the $40,000 you have at the age of 65 has the buying power of $20,000 when you are 77 and $10,000 when you are 89. That is, a 65-year-old would need $80,000 at the age of 77 to buy the same goods he bought at the age of 65 for $40,000. At a 6 percent rate of inflation, he would need $160,000 at the age of 89 to pay for the same goods he bought at the age of 65 for $40,000.

Inflation is a problem to manage. The first step toward resolution is understanding how to use your 401(k) effectively.

With a 401(k), it is up to you to choose when and how much of your earnings to set aside in your plan. You also decide how to invest (and how and when to withdraw from your plan).

As a 401(k) participant, you have to think of yourself as a long-term investor. Your investments will usually be limited to a number of investment options your company has selected for the plan. Typically, you will have a number of mutual funds to choose from, a money market fund, and possibly your company's stock.

In order to be successful, you need a set of objectives to guide your investment activity. Define your objectives in terms of where you want to be in retirement. A good starting point is: "I intend to accumulate sufficient 401(k) assets to pay myself a satisfactory monthly income throughout my retirement."

The amount you will be able to pay yourself from your 401(k) will depend more on what you do now than on what you do later. You will see the reason behind this statement in Chapter 2 when we discuss the benefits of a 401(k).

The size of your 401(k) will depend on how much time you have left before you retire and the choices you make along the way. Your 401(k) can supplement your other sources of retirement income, or it can fully fill the gap between what you will need and what you will get from Social Security and your pension. While this may be hard to fathom, *in optimal cases*, depending on how generous your company match, how soon and the extent to which you participate, and your investment choices, you could have more income from your 401(k), after taxes, than you make in the final years of employment before you retire.

Your 401(k) offers tremendous advantages over other options available to you as a saver or investor. As you begin to see these advantages, you will begin to appreciate the contribution your 401(k) can make to securing a sound financial future for you and your family.

2

How to Use the 10 Unique Advantages of a 401(k) to Far Surpass Any Other Investment Alternative

The 401(k) is designed to give you 10 advantages over any other investment alternative you might consider to grow your capital for retirement. You will need a large asset base to create a sufficient income stream for 20, 30, or more years of retirement.

No other investment alternative is better at helping you secure financial independence. By building a base of retirement assets in your 401(k) plan you can pay yourself a stream of "pension" checks throughout retirement.

As you read through the 401(k)'s 10 unique advantages, notice that the first six drive your results. These are what I call the six compounding elements of the 401(k), which derive from the way 401(k)s are designed. Compounding is the mathematical phenomenon that affects rates of growth over time — it is the multiplier effect. All other things being equal, the more compounding elements there are at work for you, the greater your rate of growth over long periods of time.

Notice that the first four advantages offer immediate compounding, which means that you benefit from immediate growth without the need to wait. I know of no investment alternative to the 401(k) that provides you with up to four immediate compounding elements.

1. **Pretax Advantage, giving you more to invest.** Earnings that you elect to contribute to the 401(k) *are not subject to current income taxes.* If the money were paid to you directly, you would have to pay income taxes on it before you invested, leaving you with less to invest. This is what is meant by pretax or before-tax savings. (The law limits how much you can set aside in pretax contributions to your plan. Some plans allow employees to make additional after-tax contributions above and beyond the maximum permitted pretax contributions. You'll read more about these issues in Chapter 12.)

2. **Leveraged Paycheck, buying you extra 401(k) dollars.** An important concept to understand about your 401(k) is that Uncle Sam is forgoing some income tax revenue on your earnings in order to help you fund your plan. I will show you how this works later in the chapter. But for now, you need to know that the dollar amount that goes into your plan as an employee contribution *is actually higher than the dollar amount that comes out of your paycheck as a payroll deduction.* The difference is due to taxes you normally would have had to pay if you were not participating in the 401(k). This is a unique benefit afforded 401(k) participants by the tax laws.

3. **Match Advantage: A special bonus from your company for participating in your plan.** Some companies will pay you a special "bonus" for participating in the plan, which is yours to keep if you stay with the company long enough to vest. In some cases, vesting is immediate. Some companies match what you contribute 25 cents on the dollar, 50 cents on the dollar, dollar for dollar, or even two dollars for every dollar you contribute. Others might pay a profit-sharing contribution instead of or in addition to the match. These special bonuses may be paid into your 401(k) account in cash or in the form of company stock. You can see that the Match

Advantage is a very important benefit. *This benefit is not available in any other type of investment alternative you might consider.*

4. **Leveraged Match: Because of special tax treatment, your "bonus" goes further.** Company matches and profit-sharing contributions are paid into your 401(k) account in full. That is, *they are not reduced by current income taxes.* If the match were paid to you directly, you would have to pay current income taxes, leaving you less to invest.

5. **Tax-Deferred Growth: You don't have to share your current investment earnings and gains with Uncle Sam.** You pay *no current income taxes on dividends, capital gains, and interest*, if any, earned in the account. This type of tax treatment is also found in other tax-deferred accounts, such as IRAs.

6. **Reinvestment Privilege: The earnings on your investments are reinvested.** Finally, as with every longer-term investment, the reinvestment of dividends, capital gains, and interest, if any, operates *to compound the initial investment.* You find this phenomenon at work in a regular investment account held for the long term.

7. **Prescreened Investment Options.** As a 401(k) participant, your investment choices are prescreened by your employer. *This makes your job as an investor much more manageable.* Your job is to understand the characteristics of each of your investment choices and to pick those that will help you reach your goals. I will teach you how to do that.

8. **Payroll Deductions, letting you save painlessly.** Advances in medicine, nutrition, and general standards of living have created an environment in which people need to have substantial assets dedicated for retirement. They will need these assets to create an income stream for periods extending long beyond their working years. Most people are well-intentioned when it comes to taking care of themselves and their families. Sometimes, however, it is difficult to keep priorities in perspective. With payroll deductions, *you can*

fund your 401(k) automatically, each pay period, without any thought or effort.

9. **Lower Taxes at tax time.** In addition to all the tax advantages discussed above, at the end of the year, *your current tax bill will be lower*, because your contribution to your 401(k) is not counted by the IRS for income-tax purposes.

10. **Postretirement Tax Advantages: You can continue tax advantages after you are ready to withdraw from your 401(k).** When you retire and need to withdraw from your 401(k), you have a number of options available to you that will allow you to *keep your income high and your taxes low.* I will illustrate these options for you in later chapters.

The real potential of the 401(k) derives from the first six advantages, the compounding elements: (1) Pretax Advantage, (2) Leveraged Paycheck, (3) Match Advantage, (4) Leveraged Match, (5) Tax-Deferred Growth, and (6) Reinvestment Privilege. Each of these characteristics drives the growth potential of a 401(k). All other things being equal, the more compounding elements there are at work for you, the greater your rate of growth.

In a 401(k) you have *both immediate and long-term compounding.* Immediate compounding is a highly desirable but rare investment characteristic that grows your investment immediately, without the need for time to pass. In the case of your 401(k), immediate compounding involves no market risk. The first four compounding elements, Pretax Advantage, Leveraged Paycheck, Match Advantage, and Leveraged Match, offer immediate compounding, by operation of the tax laws as well as the company's desire to assist you in funding your retirement. In addition, they trigger compounding elements five and six, Tax-Deferred Growth and Reinvestment Privilege, which offer the potential for long-term compounding.

The fifth and sixth factors, Tax-Deferred Growth and Reinvestment Privilege, are also available in other types of tax-advantaged investment accounts, such as IRAs. No alternative available to investors offers all six.

The extent to which you benefit from immediate compounding depends on your making correct *contribution* decisions. The extent to which you benefit from the potential for long-term compounding depends on your making correct *investment* decisions. As you read through the next eight chapters, you will begin to see how to effectively make both types of decisions.

Before retirement you will be able to use all six compounding elements to full advantage. After retirement, you lose the benefit of the first four compounding effects. However, the two remaining effects can be used to your advantage for the next 30 years or so into retirement, or even after death should your beneficiary so desire. The portion of your funds that you do not withdraw will continue to grow on a tax-deferred basis, and you will continue to reinvest dividends and capital gains.

The effect of the compounding elements in a 401(k) is best understood in comparison to a non–tax-deferred account, which I will call a "regular" account. Think of a typical bank savings account as a regular account. Your non-IRA mutual fund or brokerage account is also a regular account for our purposes.

You will see how the compounding elements work in the examples that follow.

There are some very basic things you have to know about compounding. For one, you have to remember that *time* drives the compounding effect to maximum levels. The first dollar you invest will multiply the most. The last dollar you invest will multiply the least.

To illustrate, let's look at one dollar of your earnings invested each year for 10 years at 10 percent in a 401(k) with a dollar-for-dollar match. With all six compounding elements working for you, the $10 you invested over 10 years in your 401(k) would have multiplied over and over again, due to the combined operation of the Pretax Advantage, Leveraged Paycheck, Match Advantage, Leveraged Match, Tax-Deferred Growth, and Reinvestment Privilege.

In your 401(k):

In 20 years, your $10 multiplied 9 times to $90.
In 30 years, your $10 multiplied 20 times to $200.
In 40 years, your $10 multiplied 60 times to $600.

Lacking five of the six compounding elements of the 401(k), in a regular account, the same $10 of earnings would multiply at a much slower rate. In a regular account:

In 20 years, your $10 multiplied only 3 times to $30.
In 30 years, your $10 multiplied only 5 times to $50.
In 40 years, your $10 multiplied only 10 times to $100.

The graph below shows the growth rates of both accounts used in our example, with the higher curve indicating the 401(k) investment. The assumed tax rate is 25 percent.

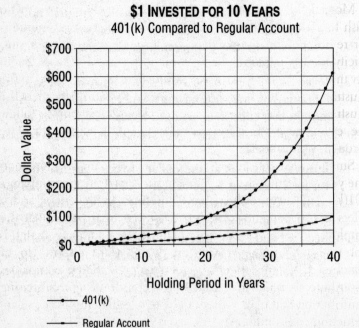

$1 INVESTED FOR 10 YEARS
401(k) Compared to Regular Account

Either case illustrates the value of time in the compounding equation. However, as you can see, the added compounding elements of the 401(k) increase growth dramatically, all other things being equal.

To demonstrate how the 10 401(k) advantages might work in your plan, I will introduce Holly to you at the age of 25 and show you how she might use her plan through the age of 90. No matter what your age, you will see how a 401(k) might work from the time you enroll through the time you withdraw money to live on in retirement, after paying taxes on the withdrawals.

In order to illustrate the advantages of a 401(k) over a regular account, I will show you Holly's 401(k) contributions, her company's matches, and her salary increases, and compare them to a regular account over time. I will keep the math to a minimum. As you read along, compare your own plan to Holly's, but refrain from making any decisions regarding your plan until you take in the information in Chapters 3 through 9.

More detail is provided in Appendix A for those of you who wish to compare different scenarios using different assumptions for returns, company matches, and taxes. For the sake of simplicity, we have not included payroll deductions for Social Security under the Federal Insurance Contributions Act (FICA) in the illustrations. These deductions would not meaningfully affect the illustrations. Unless otherwise noted, in order to help you follow the examples more easily we assume a 25 percent tax rate throughout this book.

Since Holly has been employed by her company for more than one year, full-time, she is eligible to participate in the company's 401(k). The name of her plan is the XYZ Savings Plan, and it offers a 100 percent company match up to 6 percent of the employee's pretax contribution. (This level of company match is not unusual, although there are many plans offering lower matches and some offering higher matches. Some companies contribute no match at all. Still others contribute a profit-sharing contribution that may or may not be tied to the employee's salary reduction contribution.)

Six investment options are offered by Holly's plan: a money market mutual fund, a balanced fund, a corporate bond fund, a stock index fund, a growth fund, and an international fund. (The glossary contains definitions of these terms.)

Holly currently makes $26,000 a year. Her weekly earnings are $500, before taxes. Assuming Holly's tax rate is 25 percent, $125 is withheld from her earnings, leaving her $375 each paycheck.

Holly's Weekly Earnings	$500
Taxes Withheld (25%)	−$125
Holly's Weekly Paycheck	$375

When Holly enrolls in the plan, she chooses to contribute 6 percent of her salary to her pretax 401(k) account in order to take full advantage of the company match. She chooses her investments as follows: 80 percent in the stock index fund and 20 percent in the growth fund. When she submits her enrollment form to her human resources department, a number of things are put into motion, automatically.

First, the payroll department notes Holly's contribution as a reduction of her taxable earnings. She does not pay income taxes on the amounts she is directing to be paid into her 401(k). If this were a regular investment account, she would have had to pay taxes first, leaving her less to invest. This illustrates the first compounding element, the Pretax Advantage. I will show you a mathematical illustration of the comparison in the next section.

Second, the payroll department reduces Holly's weekly salary by 6 percent and directs that amount be delivered to the plan's trustee in Holly's name. Her weekly paycheck is reduced by the amount of her pretax contribution *and adjusted for income taxes*.

It is important that you understand how the adjustment works. As shown in the table below, Holly's W-2 earnings for the weekly pay period ($500) are reduced by her contribution ($30), making her taxable earnings $470 and her withholding for taxes $117.50 (25 percent). This leaves her a paycheck of $352.50.

If you think about the significance of this payroll adjustment, you will see that $30 is going into her 401(k), but less than $30 is coming out of her paycheck. Because of the tax adjustment, the IRS is partially funding Holly's pretax contribution. This illustrates the second compounding element, Leveraged Paycheck. When you have a Leveraged Paycheck, you can "buy" your 401(k) investments at a "discount."

Stop for a minute and follow the calculations in the table below. Understanding the logic behind Holly's numbers will prepare you to do your own calculations at the end of the chapter, which will position you to take full advantage of the benefits of your 401(k).

Notice Holly's paycheck before enrollment and compare it to her paycheck after enrollment in her 401(k). Notice that Holly's contribution of $30 actually costs her $22.50 in terms of a paycheck reduction. (I call this the out-of-pocket cost of her investment through the rest of this chapter.) If you wish to compare your current out-of-pocket cost of investment, complete the table provided at the end of this chapter.

	401(K)	BEFORE ENROLLMENT
Earnings	$500.00	$500.00
Employee Contribution (6%)	−$30.00	$0.00
W-2 Earnings for Income Taxes	$470.00	$500.00
Income Taxes Withheld (25%)	−$117.50	−$125.00
Paycheck	**$352.50**	**$375.00**
Pretax Employee Contribution	**$30.00**	**$0.00**
Before Enrollment Paycheck Reduced by	**$22.50**	**$0.00**
Out-of-Pocket Cost of Investment (4.5%)	**$22.50**	**$0.00**

- ◼ *Did you notice the amount of Holly's contribution?*
  (Answer: $30.)
- ◼ *Did you notice how much of her paycheck was used to fund the contribution?*
  (Answer: Only $22.50. Holly's "discount" was $7.50 or 25%.)

Where did this come from? Compare Holly's paycheck before she enrolled and after she enrolled. Her paycheck before enrollment was $375. Her paycheck after enrollment was $352.50. The difference, $22.50, is the amount by which Holly's paycheck was reduced in order to fund the $30 contribution.

■ *How much did Holly's contribution of $30 cost her?*
(Answer: $22.50. Holly's $30 contribution to her 401(k) cost her only $22.50, the amount by which her paycheck was reduced. This illustrates the second compounding element, Leveraged Paycheck.)

Because of the immediate compounding effect of Leveraged Paycheck, you can see that Holly is "buying" her 401(k) investment at a "discount." That is, she is "buying" her $30 investment at $22.50, which is a "discount" of 25 percent. You can use this advantage to grow your 401(k) much faster than you could a regular account and still be ahead when you pay taxes on your withdrawals if you plan your retirement distribution strategy wisely. As you will see on page 36, your discount will be higher if your plan provides a company match.

In order to fully understand the significance of the Pretax Advantage and the Leveraged Paycheck, you have to compare a 401(k) with a regular account. These are important concepts to understand in order to fully appreciate how much of an advantage your 401(k) gives you over any other investment vehicle.

The question becomes, *in a regular account, how much would Holly's $30 contribution cost her?* The answer is $40. That is, assuming a 25 percent tax rate, to put $30 of your earnings in a regular account, you need to earn enough to pay the government 25 cents on the dollar and have $30 left over to invest.

That relationship sets up the following problem to solve. Assume that $30 equals 75 percent, which is your share of your paycheck, and solve for 25 percent, the government's share. Twenty-five percent is one-third of 75 percent. One-third of $30 is $10. Therefore the government's share is $10. In order to pay yourself $30 (75 percent) and the government $10 (25 percent), you need to earn $40 (100 percent).

	401(K)	REGULAR ACCOUNT
Credited to Investment Account	$30.00	$30.00
Out-of-Pocket Cost of Investment	$22.50	$40.00

- *How much would Holly's pretax 401(k) contributions total over a year?*
  (Answer: $1,560 [$30 × 52 = $1,560].)
- *In a regular account, how much would Holly's $1,560 contribution cost her (No Pretax Advantage)?*
  (Answer: $2,080 [$40 × 52 = $2,080]. Please refer to the discussion above to see how to arrive at the $40 figure.)
- *How much would Holly's annual pretax 401(k) contribution of $1,560 cost her (Leveraged Paycheck)?*
  (Answer: Only $1,170 [$22.50 × 52 = $1,170].)

	401(K)	REGULAR ACCOUNT
Credited to Investment Account	$1,560	$1,560
Out-of-Pocket Cost of Investment	$1,170	$2,080

When you compare a regular account, you can see that your earnings go much further in a 401(k) because of the Pretax Advantage. In a regular account you have to earn $2,080 ($40 for every $30 you want to invest), assuming a 25 percent tax rate. Because of the Pretax Advantage, you only have to earn $30 to fund $30 of 401(k) contribution.

When you add the effect of the Leveraged Paycheck, your 401(k) comes out even further ahead, since your $30 of earnings are not taken out of your paycheck in full, due to tax adjustments. As a result, you pay only $22.50 for every $30 invested, getting $1,560 worth of 401(k) with only $1,170 of your earnings.

Third, the payroll department allocates the company match. Since the match is 100 percent, the company puts $30 into Holly's company match account with respect to each pay period. The match is really a "bonus" the company pays you to participate in the plan. This illustrates the third compounding element, the Match Advantage.

■ *Now, with her match, how much has Holly accumulated in a week?*
    (Answer: $60. [$30 company match plus her $30 contribution.])
■ *How much has Holly's paycheck been reduced?*
    (Answer: $22.50 came out of her paycheck, but her account is credited almost three times as much: $60.)
■ *How does this compare to her regular account?*
    (Answer: In her regular account, no one matches her contribution and her account is credited only her original $30, which actually cost her $40 of earnings.)

	401(K)	REGULAR ACCOUNT
Employee Contribution	$30.00	$30.00
Company Match	$30.00	$0.00
Credited to Investment Account	$60.00	$30.00
Out-of-Pocket Cost of Investment	$22.50	$40.00

■ *How much will Holly's take-home pay for the year be affected, compared to how much goes into her account?*

(Answer: $1,170 [$22.50 × 52] comes out of her paychecks, but her account is credited almost three times as much: $3,120 [$60 × 52].)

	401(K)	REGULAR ACCOUNT
Employee Contribution	$1,560	$1,560
Company Match	$0	$0
Credited to Investment Account	$3,120	$1,560
Out-of-Pocket Cost of Investment	$1,170	$2,080

This illustrates the power of the addition of a third compounding element, the Match Advantage. Holly's $1,170 compounded to $3,120, even before she started investing. Looking at it another way, Holly was able to "buy" $3,120 worth of her 401(k) investment for only $1,170, a "discount" of more than 62 percent. Remember that the IRS will want to get its share of revenues from Holly at the time she begins withdrawing from her 401(k) in retirement. However, as you will see in Chapter 10, the IRS provides you the means of keeping taxes to a minimum by stretching out withdrawals over your lifetime.

Fourth, the match is not taxed as income to you and does not appear on your W-2. This is the fourth compounding element, Leveraged Match.

■ *How much does Holly pay in current income taxes on her company match?*
(Answer: Nothing. Her company match does not appear on Holly's W-2 for income tax purposes.)

You can see the dramatic effect of the first four compounding elements when you compare a 401(k) to a regular account over a long period of time. Let's look at Holly's contributions over 40 years and the difference between Holly's 401(k) and a regular account. For purposes of this comparison, Holly's salary contributions are kept at a constant $30 a week as in the above examples, in order for you to be able to follow the calculations easily. Also for the sake of simplicity, the tax rate is kept at a constant 25 percent throughout the period. Later, I will add a higher tax rate assumption.

As you will see from the discussion and table that follow, there are two significant consequences of the first four compounding effects. First, you need to spend less to buy more. Second, your account grows without exposure to market risk.

In 40 years, Holly contributed $62,400 of her earnings to her 401(k) ($1,560 × 40 = $62,400), but because of her 401(k) Leveraged Paycheck, her actual cost was only $46,800 ($1,170 × 40 = $46,800). Because of the effect of the Pretax Advantage, Leveraged Paycheck, Match Advantage, and Leveraged Match, her $46,800 grew to $124,800, before investment. Holly was able to leverage $46,800 into $124,800 without any market risk.

There are no compounding effects in play in Holly's regular account at this level of analysis. Because of the absence of the Pretax Advantage, in order to invest $124,800 (75 percent), Holly would have to earn $166,400 (100 percent) to pay the government its 25 percent share ($41,600) in income taxes. As a result, Holly would have to earn $166,400 to pay for her $124,800 investment in a regular account, which would cost her only $46,800 in her 401(k). Now that four of the compounding effects are in play, Holly is able to "buy" $124,800 of 401(k) investments at a bargain price of only $46,800 of her earnings, a "discount" of 62.5 percent.

	401(K)	REGULAR ACCOUNT
Employee Contribution Over 40 Years	$62,400	$124,800
Company Match	$62,400	$0
Credited to Investment Account	**$124,800**	**$124,800**
Out-of-Pocket Cost of Investment	**$46,800**	**$166,400**

You can see that the Pretax Advantage is a particularly powerful compounding tool, which, taken together with the Leveraged Paycheck, Match Advantage, and Leveraged Match, results in compounding effects that put you ahead without market risk. You can imagine how much more the account might grow with the fifth and sixth compounding effects in play.

Fifth, any dividends, capital gains, or interest paid on any of her 401(k) investment account, including her pretax, after-tax, and company match account, will not be taxed until Holly takes her money out of her 401(k), normally in retirement. This is what is meant by the term "tax deferral." This is the fifth compounding element, Tax-Deferred Growth, and it is driven by the first four compounding elements. That is, your Pretax Advantage, Leveraged Paycheck, Match Advantage, and Leveraged Match will feed both the fifth and sixth compounding elements, Tax-Deferred Growth and Reinvestment Privilege.

If Holly had invested in a regular account, any investments that generated dividends, interest, or capital gains would be subject to current taxation. She would know how much would be due in taxes when she received a Form 1099-Div, or Form 1099-Int, from her bank, brokerage firm, or mutual fund.

Holly will not receive a 1099 from her 401(k) plan until distribution, normally in retirement. Neither will Holly have to pay capital gains tax on any gains she might make on the sale of any of her investment holdings in her 401(k) (a "sale" includes an "exchange" from one fund to another). Holly does not need to keep track of purchase and sales prices at all, since she will not have to account for capital gains on individual investment holdings in her 401(k). (I will show you how taxes are accounted for at the time of withdrawal at the end of this chapter and in Chapter 10. Additional tax issues are discussed in Chapter 12.)

Sixth, all the money in Holly's 401(k) — her own contributions and her company's match — is invested in accordance with her directions on the enrollment form. The characteristics of her chosen investments will determine the amounts of dividends, interest, or capital gains distributions, if any, as well as the expected risks and potential rewards of the holdings. Usually the investments are purchased by the plan administrator once a month, after the payroll department provides the administrator a list of all participants in the plan and the amounts they are directing to be invested. The investment and reinvestment of dividends, capital gains, and interest, if any, is the sixth compounding element, the Reinvestment Privilege.

To illustrate the difference between the 401(k) and a regular account over a long period of time, let's look at Holly's 40-year experience, from age 25 to age 65.

The following table shows you the differences between the two types of accounts. In this example, I am showing $30 a week invested for 40 years as in the earlier example. In this case, however, the employee contribution for the regular account does not include an extra investment on Holly's part to cover what she would have received in a match. The tables do not show any increases in Holly's salary or in her contributions. In Appendix A, I will show you other tables that do take into account cost of living adjustments, which would increase the amount she is investing and the ending value of her accounts. In each case below, I am assuming a total return of 10 percent per year. Appendix A shows some different return scenarios, which include actual market experience. Your return on your 401(k) will depend on your investment selections.

	401(K)	REGULAR ACCOUNT
Employee Contribution Over 40 Years	$62,400	$62,400
Company Match	$62,400	$0
Total Investment	$124,800	$62,400
Total Out-of-Pocket Cost of Investment	$46,800	$83,200
Total Value of Account at Age 65 (10% Rate of Return)	$1,500,000	$285,000

From the table you can see the dramatic divergence between the 401(k) and the regular account and the powerful effect of the six compounding factors allowed to work to their fullest. Over the 40-year period, Holly's cost of investing in her 401(k) was only $46,800, and by the end of the period, her account had grown to $1.5 million.

In comparison, Holly's cost of investing in her regular account was $83,200. Because only one compounding element was at work in her regular account, her regular account grew to only $285,000. That is, Holly needed to earn $83,200 in order to invest $62,400 to get $285,000 by age 65.

■ *How much was Holly's 401(k) account ahead over her regular account, even though it was invested in exactly the same way?* (Answer: Her 401(k) was ahead by $1,215,000 [$1,500,000 − $285,000].)

Holly's 401(k) grew so much more than her regular account because her 401(k) had six compounding factors working for it. Her regular account only had one compounding factor working for it, and there were taxes to pay along the way. (In this example, the assumed rate of return is 10 percent and the holding period is 40 years, but there are no adjustments for salary increases Holly would have received along the way. Holly's actual 401(k) experience would have been better if salary increases were included, since they translate into increased 401(k) contributions. If Holly's return had been lower and her holding period shorter, the difference between the two accounts would have been less dramatic.)

Some of you might say there will be a big price to pay for all these 401(k) advantages when you retire. Let's look at what happens if you take all your money out in one lump sum at the age of 65 and pay taxes on the withdrawal in full at two different tax rates: the 25 percent tax rate we have been using in our examples and a 45 percent tax rate. This method of withdrawal is the worst case scenario for our illustration. Later, I will show you examples of other withdrawal methods you can use to lower your taxes and continue your tax deferral past retirement, so that you can pay yourself a satisfactory after-tax "pension" check in retirement out of your 401(k). The following is the worst-case tax scenario, a full lump sum withdrawal at age 65, without a rollover. First, we'll look at a 25 percent tax rate:

	401(K)	REGULAR ACCOUNT
Employee Contribution Over 40 Years	$62,400	$62,400
Company Match	$62,400	$0
Total Investment	$124,800	$62,400
Total Out-of-Pocket Cost of Investment	**$46,800**	**$83,200**
Total Value of Account at Age 65 (10% Rate of Return)	$1,500,000	$285,000
Taxes Assuming 100% Withdrawal at 65 (Rate: 25%)	$375,000	$0
Account Value After Tax of 25%	**$1,125,000**	**$285,000**

Now, let's assume Holly's tax rate jumps to 45 percent at age 65:

	401(K)	REGULAR ACCOUNT
Taxes Assuming 100% Withdrawal at 65 (Rate: 45%)	$675,000	$0
Account Value After Tax of 45%	**$825,000**	**$285,000**

No matter what amount of time you look at, your 401(k) will give you an advantage over a regular account if all six compounding factors are at work. The longer you have, of course, the greater the potential benefits. (If your plan does not provide a Match Advantage or Leveraged Match, you will have to assess whether your other four compounding elements will be sufficient for your 401(k) to give you an advantage over a regular account. In most cases I have seen, they do, by far.)

Seventh, when Holly needed to decide her investment choices, she worked with a list given to her by her company as part of the enrollment package. There were six investment options to choose from. Holly studied the six options and determined which investments she felt were best suited for her in light of her goal to accumulate retirement assets over the rest of her working life. Her job was made easier for her because her company had already looked at the universe of investment vehicles available and determined the six it thought best to provide for its employees. This is the seventh 401(k) advantage, Prescreened Investment Options. Your investment decisions will determine the effectiveness of your fifth and sixth compounding factors, Tax-Deferred Growth and Reinvestment Privilege. In Holly's examples so far, we have been using a 10 percent rate of return. The return you will achieve will depend on your investment choices. Other rates of return are shown in Appendix A.

Eighth, every pay period, Holly's paycheck reflects a contribution to her 401(k). She doesn't have to do anything to continue her contributions. This is how the eighth 401(k) advantage, saving painlessly through Payroll Deductions, works.

Ninth, at the end of the year, payroll sends Holly a W-2, putting in motion the ninth 401(k) advantage, Lower Taxes.

Remember Holly's salary? It was $26,000. Her company match was an additional $30-a-week bonus, bringing her earnings up to $27,560. What will her W-2 show? $27,560? $26,000? $24,440?

The amounts Holly contributes to her 401(k) are not included on her W-2 for income taxes, and neither are the amounts her company contributes to her account as a match. Specifically, Holly's company reports Holly's annual earnings to the IRS as only $24,440, which is $26,000 minus her pretax contributions of $1,560 for the year.

Tenth, Holly can continue her tax deferrals beyond retirement because of another tax law benefit for 401(k)s. Earlier, you saw the tax effect of a lump-sum withdrawal at the age of 65. There is no need to pay these taxes. One of the advantages of a 401(k) is the ability to continue tax-deferred growth throughout retirement, if desired, as long as you start minimum mandatory taxable withdrawals at age 70½.

In Chapter 10, I will go through withdrawal scenarios available to you in retirement. For the time being, let me show you some numbers using a withdrawal method called the "recalculating" method assuming that Holly wants to continue to grow her account until the age of 70½, when she is required by law to begin mandatory distributions. The recalculating method is one of the methods of withdrawal permitted by the IRS to continue tax deferral of your 401(k) into retirement, while withdrawing (and paying taxes on) minimum amounts each year.

From the age of 65 through age 71, Holly will be rebalancing her portfolio from capital growth holdings into income-producing instruments. We have assumed a rate of return of 6 percent for this period. Her actual returns will depend on the markets.

In our earlier example, Holly's salary and contributions were not increased over time. She contributed $46,800 over 40 years, and her account compounded to $1.5 million by the age of 65. From the age of 65 through age 71, the account grew at a 6 percent rate to over $2 million. Beginning at age 71, she took minimum withdrawals and paid taxes on those withdrawals. Using the recalculating method, Holly would have withdrawn over $2 million, after taxes, over the 20-year period between the ages of 71 and 91, and she would have $500,000 left at age 91.

In comparison, Holly would have withdrawn only $472,500 from her regular account over the same period, and she would have $375,000 left at age 91. Please remember that Holly's actual returns will depend on market returns, which fluctuate. These numbers are static and are being used solely to illustrate how a withdrawal strategy might work in a 401(k) in comparison to a regular account.

It must be emphasized that the differences between the 401(k) and the regular account are not due to taking on extra risk. Both accounts are invested in the same way. The dramatic differences come solely from the operation of the compounding elements of the 401(k), given a long period of time to develop.

The different ways in which you can manage your taxes at the time of withdrawal are discussed in Chapter 10, where I will show you additional scenarios showing different assumptions.

For now, you can see how a 401(k) might give you the potential for gaining momentum in your savings due to the 10 advantages described in this chapter. You can see that in optimal cases such as Holly's, the 401(k) can produce after-tax income in retirement that far surpasses preretirement paychecks.

You might wish to see how your 401(k) plan compares to Holly's. At this point, you might begin gathering some information about your plan. Calculate your effective tax rate, and, if you are currently participating in your 401(k), determine your current pretax contribution, your current after-tax contribution, and details on your company match or profit sharing contribution.

The table below will help you calculate your effective tax rate. Look at your most recent tax returns and insert the following figures into the table.

TAX RATE TABLE

1. Gross Income (insert from federal income tax return): ☐
2. Federal Income Taxes Paid (insert from federal income tax return): ☐
3. State Income Taxes Paid (insert from state income tax return, if any): ☐
4. Total Income Taxes Paid (Line 2 plus Line 3): ☐
5. Effective Tax Rate (Line 4 divided by Line 1): ☐

You will use your effective tax rate throughout this book as a very rough measure of the overall impact of income taxes on your 401(k) account for comparison to your regular account.

The following table will help you quantify your Leveraged Paycheck and compare it to how much is actually going into your 401(k) from your salary reduction. This information may lead you to check whether your withholding should be increased. Before changing your level of contribution, wait until you've read Chapters 3, 4 and 5.

By filling in the table, you will be able to see how much of a 401(k) contribution you can "buy at a discount," due strictly to your Leveraged Paycheck. You will also see how your paycheck will be adjusted. If your plan offers a match or a profit-sharing contribution, you will get an additional "discount" that you will be able to compare in the table on page 78. First, I'll show you an example of a filled-in table and then I'll provide you with a blank table for you to complete.

BENEFIT OF LEVERAGED PAYCHECK TABLE (EXAMPLE)

	BEFORE PARTICIPATION	AFTER PARTICIPATION
1. Insert Earnings for Pay Period	$3,000	$3,000
2. Pretax Contribution	− $0	− $180
3. W-2 Earnings for Income Taxes (Line 1 − Line 2)	= $3,000	= $2,820
4. Insert Your Effective Tax Rate (%) (from Tax Rate Table)	× 25.00%	× 25.00%
5. Income Taxes Withheld (Line 3 × Line 4)	= $750	= $705

Net Take-Home Pay

6. Insert Earnings for Pay Period (same as Line 1)	$3,000	$3,000
7. Pretax Contribution (same as Line 2)	− $0	− $180
8. Income Taxes Withheld (same as Line 5)	− $750	− $705
9. **Net Take-Home Pay** (Line 6 − Lines 7 and 8)	= $2,250	= $2,115

Out-of-Pocket Cost (Considering Only Leveraged Paycheck)

10. Difference in Net Take-Home Pay, Before and After Participating (Line 9 Before − Line 9 After) $135

Benefit of Leveraged Paycheck

11. Amount of 401(k) Benefit (same as Line 2) $180

12. Out-of-Pocket Cost of Your Investment (same as Line 10) $135

13. Amount by Which You Are Ahead, Before Match and Investments (Line 11 − Line 12)   = $45

BENEFIT OF LEVERAGED PAYCHECK TABLE
(BLANK FOR YOU TO FILL IN)

	BEFORE PARTICIPATION	AFTER PARTICIPATION
1. Insert Earnings for Pay Period	☐	☐
2. Pretax Contribution	− $0	− ☐
3. W-2 Earnings for Income Taxes (Line 1 − Line 2)	= ☐	= ☐
4. Insert Your Effective Tax Rate (%) (from Tax Rate Table)	× ☐ %	× ☐ %
5. Income Taxes Withheld (Line 3 × Line 4)	= ☐	= ☐

Net Take-Home Pay

	BEFORE PARTICIPATION	AFTER PARTICIPATION
6. Insert Earnings for Pay Period (same as Line 1)	☐	☐
7. Pretax Contribution (same as Line 2)	− $0	− ☐
8. Income Taxes Withheld (same as Line 5)	− ☐	− ☐
9. **Net Take-Home Pay** (Line 6 − Lines 7 and 8)	= ☐	= ☐

Out-of-Pocket Cost (Considering Only Leveraged Paycheck)

10. Difference in Net Take-Home Pay, Before and After Participating (Line 9 Before − Line 9 After)   ☐

Benefit of Leveraged Paycheck

11. Amount of 401(k) Benefit (same as Line 2)   ☐

12. Out-of-Pocket Cost of Your Investment (same as Line 10)   ☐

13. Amount by Which You Are Ahead, Before Match and Investments (Line 11 − Line 12)   = ☐

3

The Seven Key Features
of a 401(k)

In order to offer all the benefits discussed in Chapter 2 of this book, your employer has to comply with a number of very specific legal requirements qualifying your savings plan for 401(k) tax advantages. It is these requirements, together with the economic decisions of offering the 401(k), that shape the elements of your particular plan. There is some flexibility in what your employer can provide in the plan, particularly in terms of matching, which will be discussed below.

In Chapters 1 and 2, I introduced some of the common features of the 401(k). In this chapter, I will get into more detail, to provide you with a frame of reference about what you might find in your plan. In later chapters, I will direct you to your plan with specific questions that you will need to have answered before you start making choices called for by your plan.

Generally, most plans provide the following seven key features, some of which are essential and some of which are optional. You will need to read your plan summary or plan document to determine the characteristics of the plan your company provides.

- *Your Pretax Contributions.* An essential element of any 401(k) plan is the ability for an eligible employee to make a pretax contribution to the plan through payroll deductions. All 401(k) plans must provide for a direction from you to your employer to deduct a certain percentage or dollar amount of your earnings to fund your elective pretax account. The amounts you so direct will appear on a statement issued to you periodically by your plan administrator, as will all the following categories. Your pretax contributions offer you two compounding elements, the Pretax Advantage and the Leveraged Paycheck.

- *Your After-Tax Contributions.* Some plans also allow you to direct your employer to place a certain percentage of your after-tax earnings in an after-tax account. After-tax contributions offer you two compounding elements, Tax-Deferred Growth and the Reinvestment Privilege.

- *Company Match.* While your employer is not required by law to contribute to the plan, many companies do match your pretax or after-tax contributions, or both, partially, fully, or more. Your company match is of utmost importance to understand. Your match offers you two compounding elements, Match Advantage and Leveraged Match.

- *Investment Choices.* The whole purpose behind providing a 401(k) to employees is to help them invest for the future. Almost every plan provides a selection of investment options for the employee to choose from. Your investment choices determine your long-term compounding, and offer you two compounding elements, Tax-Deferred Growth and the Reinvestment Privilege.

- *Loans.* Some plans allow you to borrow from your account. If there is a loan provision, the plan must provide that you repay the loan within five years, unless the loan is for the purchase of your principal residence. Loans should be approached with caution, especially if you are changing employers. Be certain to understand your borrowing rules before you take out a loan from your 401(k).

- *Withdrawals.* Your 401(k) is an investment tool for retirement, and plan administrators are generally prohibited from disbursing funds before then. Plans may provide for exceptions in the case of financial hardship. Distributions are also allowed at retirement, death, disability, and change of employment.

- *Taxes.* Any and all withdrawals are subject to immediate income taxes, unless you roll over into another tax-deferred vehicle within 60 days of the withdrawal. This is similar to the tax treatment of an IRA. In addition, there is a penalty for early withdrawals made under the age of 59½ and 20 percent withholding for amounts not directly rolled over.

Your Pretax Contributions. It is up to you to determine how much to set aside from your earnings in your 401(k) as a pretax contribution. Your pretax contribution goes into a "pretax account" in your name. The pretax contribution is also called an "elective" contribution or a "salary reduction."

When you decide to participate in your 401(k), you will be asked to fill out an enrollment form that tells your employer to make deductions from your earnings to place in your 401(k). Five things happen when you send in the enrollment form. First, your company's payroll department is notified to reduce your paychecks in the appropriate amount. Second, the money is sent to the 401(k) custodian, who places the money into a special pretax account in your name. Third, the payroll department makes a notation that these amounts are properly reported on your W-2 so that you are not subject to income tax on them at the end of the year. Fourth, if your plan provides for a company match, the administrator of the plan calculates the amount of the match based on the amount of your pretax contribution.

Fifth, the funds are invested according to your directions. How to direct the investment of your funds is a very important decision that has a number of different elements. I will take you through the process of making those decisions in Chapters 6 through 9.

There are limits on how much you can set aside as a pretax contribution. Generally, the minimum you can set aside is 1 percent of your annual compensation. If your plan is like the majority of plans, you may make pretax contributions from a minimum of 1 percent to a maximum of 10 percent of your compensation. Some plans provide for higher maximums. You may not be able to actually set aside the maximum provided in your plan because of another set of limitations imposed by the Internal Revenue Code.

The Internal Revenue Code limitations on maximums are determined by a number of different tests, which can change from year to year. One test sets a dollar limit on the annual pretax contribution. For example, the 1996 maximum is $9,500. Another test requires all contributions, including elective, after-tax, company matches, and forfeitures to be taken into account in determining the maximum contribution permitted by law. A third test applies to highly compensated employees and requires a calculation be made based on the compensation and participation of all eligible employees.

Your employer is responsible for making certain that your pretax contributions do not exceed legal limits. The administrator of your plan performs what is called "discrimination testing" on the plan periodically to determine that the maximums are not exceeded. Should the problem of excess deferrals or contributions arise, a portion of your contribution will be refunded to you by the administrator. If the refunding needs to be done after you have received your W-2 for the year, you will receive an amended W-2 from your employer to account for the refund, or the refund will be added to the next year's W-2.

To find out the limits of your plan, ask your personnel director or human resources officer for a copy of your plan or a plan summary. If you are a highly compensated employee, you may need to speak to your plan administrator about the maximum limits that apply to you.

Your pretax contributions are fully and immediately vested and fully and immediately portable. This means that your pretax account belongs to you from the day your first contribution reaches your 401(k) plan trustee. Should you die, the account will go to your named beneficiary. Should you leave your employer, you can take the account with you.

Withdrawals of your pretax contributions are strictly limited by the tax laws. Because the purpose of a 401(k) is to help you save for retirement with tax-deferred contributions, the law prohibits you from taking pretax money out of your plan before the age of 59½ except in limited circumstances, such as death, disability, or separation from service. In addition, there is a 10 percent penalty tax on withdrawals before age 59½ except in event of death, disability, or separation from service after age 55. Chapter 12 discusses hardship withdrawals, which are also permitted, but subject to the 10 percent penalty tax.

Your After-Tax Contributions. Some plans allow you to direct your employer to place a certain percentage of your after-tax earnings in an after-tax account. Since you have already paid taxes on your after-tax contributions, these contributions do not get the full benefits that 401(k)s offer. Although not as advantageous as pretax contributions, earnings on after-tax contributions do receive tax-deferral benefits and may be matched by your employer, depending on the plan. If you have maximized your pretax contributions and are considering investing in a regular account for retirement purposes, you might first consider after-tax contributions to your 401(k) for tax-deferral benefits. You need to be aware, however, that in rare cases, the amount you contribute on an after-tax basis may lessen your company match on pretax contributions. For this reason, it is very important to understand the consequences of making after-tax contributions, particularly if you are a highly compensated employee.

Withdrawal of your pretax account is restricted by law. Withdrawal of your after-tax account is determined by the provisions of your plan. See Chapter 12 for more information on pretax and after-tax accounts.

Company Contribution. One of the decisions an employer needs to make when it is designing a 401(k) plan contribution is whether it, the company, should make its own contributions to employee accounts, and if so to what extent and in what manner. These are economic and business decisions, which turn on many factors, including the other types of benefits already provided by the company to its employees.

For some companies, compelling business reasons prevent them from contributing any money to the 401(k). If you participate in such a plan, your 401(k) will not give you the maximum compounding effects of other plans offering 50 percent, 100 percent, or 200 percent matching of your pretax contributions. Other companies match after-tax contributions as well. Some companies do not match your contributions, but instead contribute a profit-sharing bonus to your plan, the amount of which depends on how well the company is doing, without regard to how much you have contributed to the plan. Still other companies provide both a match and a profit-sharing contribution.

There are two more variables in matching. One is whether the company matches in cash or in company stock. The second is vesting. Vesting is the term that is used to indicate that the company match is yours to keep. The law requires company plans to provide for 100 percent vesting no later than five years or 20 percent each year in the third through seventh years. Consequently, depending on how your company's plan is drawn, your company match may be vesting 100 percent immediately for you to take with you should you leave your employer now. If it vests in five years, you would not be eligible to take your company match account with you until five years after you begin working for the company.

Your company plan may provide that the match is paid in cash for you to invest in accordance with the options set out in the plan. Or the company match may be paid in company stock. If the match is paid in stock, you have to be particularly careful to consider diversification of your pretax contribution and your after-tax contribution, if any, so as not to have too high a concentration in company stock. Your pretax account is kept separate from your after-tax account for tax reasons. Usually, you can direct the investment of each account differently if you wish.

As you can see, there is quite a bit of flexibility in terms of what your employer can do in the plan when it comes to company contributions. You will have to look to your plan to determine your company's policy with respect to the matching provisions of your plan.

From your perspective as a participant, any time your company provides a match, your 401(k) rises in value to you, since your ability to compound your holdings is greatly increased by the amount of the match. The most powerful 401(k)s are the ones that provide matching, profit sharing, or other company contributions.

While you cannot control whether and to what extent your plan provides contributions, you can control whether you get the maximum benefits from the match. This is an important decision for you. In Chapter 5 I will show you how to maximize your contributions so that you get the highest benefit from your match.

Investment Choices. Virtually all 401(k) plans provide a number of investment choices from which to select. How to make your investment decisions is covered in Chapters 6 through 9.

Loans. Whether you can borrow from your 401(k) is determined by the provisions of your plan. Loans are not required to be part of a 401(k) plan. By law, there are limits on the amount you can borrow, which are reflected in your plan. The plan also sets out the interest rate you will pay on amounts you borrow.

When you borrow from your 401(k) plan, you are actually borrowing from yourself. Consequently, when you pay interest on the loan, you are paying yourself. Both interest and principal payments go back into your 401(k) account.

Some companies require you to fill out a written application for a loan. Others make it easier to get a loan from your 401(k) — you just call your administrator and make an oral application. You will be asked to sign a loan agreement before a check is sent out to you. The loan agreement sets out the amount of the loan, your principal repayment schedule, the interest rate charged, your authorization to your employer to make payroll deductions for the principal and interest payments as they come due, and your spouse's consent to the loan.

When you take out your loan, your payroll stub will show the amount of your principal and interest repayment. The loan repayment amount is deducted from your pay as after-tax dollars, separate from your normal 401(k) contribution. The repayment amount goes back into your pretax or after-tax 401(k) account, depending on the origin of the loan.

Your contributions to your 401(k) are unaffected by these loan repayments. That is, your payroll stub will still show your pretax contributions and your after-tax contributions, if any. Your company matches, if any, will continue as usual. You will see all of these transactions on your 401(k) account statement. Interest payments you pay on the loan are not tax deductible, even if the loan is for the purchase of your residence, unless they qualify as investment interest or mortgage interest.

Normally, you can repay the outstanding loan amount at any time without penalty. To ensure repayment and meet the requirements of the Employee Retirement Income Security Act of 1974 (ERISA), the plan takes a security interest equal to 50 percent of your vested accounts. The plan will exercise the security interest if you fail to repay the loan. That is, if you leave the company, the loan will be immediately due and payable. If you do not repay the loan within 90 days of your last payment, the outstanding balance will be deducted from your account balance. This amount would be considered a taxable distribution from the plan subject to taxation and IRS penalties for early withdrawal if you are under the age of 59½. To avoid the penalty, you would have to repay the loan.

Whether you borrow from your plan will depend on your particular circumstances. There may be legitimate reasons to borrow from your 401(k) — for example, to fund the purchase of a residence. However, you should be very careful about taking out a loan, especially if you plan to change employers.

Withdrawals. You need to be aware of two issues when thinking of a withdrawal. First, you should not consider withdrawing from your plan except for retirement income or because of financial hardship. In all other cases, if you must take money from your account for a sound reason, consider taking a loan from your 401(k) instead. When you change employers, you may be tempted to withdraw all your 401(k), pay the penalties and taxes, and spend the remainder. Be certain to either continue your plan at your old employer, if permitted by your plan, continue your plan at your new employer, if rollovers are permitted into your new plan, or roll your money over into an IRA. It is of utmost importance to continue growing your retirement assets if at all possible.

Second, withdrawals of pretax accounts and company matches made before the age of 59½ and withdrawals of employer contributions (matches and profit sharing) before age 59½ are subject to an additional 10 percent tax penalty for early withdrawal. There are certain instances in which the penalty does not apply under the age of 59½. They are: 1) severance of service, but only if over the age of 55; 2) disability; 3) death. In all other cases, the penalty applies if you are under the age of 59½, even in the case of a hardship withdrawal. In all cases, no matter what your age or circumstances, there is always an income tax on pretax accounts and company match accounts, and in all plan earnings, but not on after-tax contributions. Please see the tables at the end of this chapter for more information on withdrawal rules and applicable penalties and taxes.

Taxes. All 401(k) plan money, except after-tax contributions, is taxed on withdrawal as income. You have the option of rolling over the taxable portion of any withdrawal into an IRA to continue to defer taxes. This is usually the desirable course of action. The rollover must occur within 60 days of withdrawal.

When it is time to take money out of your 401(k) for retirement income, you have a number of options. Mandatory withdrawals are required by law beginning at age 70½. However, you should be certain to get competent tax advice well before that time to ensure the optimum distribution approach. You can either take a full distribution and pay income taxes on the entire amount at the time of withdrawal, or take periodic payments using the recalculating method, the term-certain method, or a fixed number of installments. These methods are described in IRS publication 590 for IRAs. Taxes and distributions can be kept to a minimum with the recalculating method, but earlier-than-expected death of the participant or spouse may significantly increase taxes. See Chapter 12 for a discussion of trust and estate issues.

Any money you contribute on an after-tax basis is treated differently from pretax contributions and matches. After-tax contributions are not subject to early withdrawal penalties or income taxes.

Managing your withdrawals and your tax consequences will be an important part of how you handle your 401(k).

The seven features of 401(k)s are all described in detail in your plan summary. As you can see, it is important to become familiar with your plan's features so that you can begin to formulate a good plan of action. Knowing these features, start thinking about the following questions:

- *What do I want my 401(k) to do for me?*
- *What are the investment rules I am going to apply to my 401(k)? Include rules for withdrawals and loans.*
- *What procedures am I going to use to monitor my investments and my progress? How will I know if I am on course?*
- *How much do I need to invest to maximize the compounding elements provided in my plan?*
- *How will I achieve my 401(k) goals?*
- *What rules will I develop for myself regarding withdrawals? Will I try to limit withdrawals to retirement, except in an emergency? Will I try to limit loans to emergencies or will I use loans for other purposes?*
- *What are my current thoughts regarding handling taxes when I withdraw?*

If you make the withdrawal, is there a 10% early withdrawal penalty?
Is the withdrawal taxable as income?

NOTE: If subject to income tax, amounts can be rolled over into another tax-deferred account to avoid a current tax*

Withdrawal made when:	PRETAX EMPLOYEE CONTRIBUTIONS	AFTER-TAX EMPLOYEE CONTRIBUTIONS**	COMPANY CONTRIBUTIONS RESPECTING PRETAX OR AFTER-TAX EMPLOYEE CONTRIBUTIONS
Over Age 59½	Penalty: NO Income Tax: YES	Penalty: NO Income Tax: NO	Penalty: NO Income Tax: YES
Under Age 59½, but over 55 and separating from service	Penalty: NO Income Tax: YES	Penalty: NO Income Tax: NO	Penalty: NO Income Tax: YES
Under Age 59½, but disabled	Penalty: NO Income Tax: YES	Penalty: NO Income Tax: NO	Penalty: NO Income Tax: YES
Under Age 55, and separating from service	Penalty: YES Income Tax: YES	Penalty: NO Income Tax: NO	Penalty: YES Income Tax: YES
Under Age 59½, but requesting hardship withdrawal	Penalty: YES Income Tax: YES	Penalty: NO Income Tax: NO	Penalty: YES Income Tax: YES
Under Age 59½ at date of death	Penalty: NO Income Tax: YES	Penalty: NO Income Tax: NO	Penalty: NO Income Tax: YES

* Withdrawals and distributions eligible for rollover are subject to 20% withholding unless transferred directly into an appropriate tax-deferred account. Amounts withheld can be replaced to effect a rollover of the full amount of the distribution and avoid income taxes.

** Withdrawals from after-tax accounts include some earnings, which are treated the same as pretax contributions for penalty and income tax purposes.

	Limitations Imposed by Law	Limitations Imposed by the Plan
Pretax Employee Contributions Also called "Elective"	**Vesting:** 100% immediate vesting.	**Vesting:** 100% immediate vesting.
	Tax: Contributions are *not* included as income in W-2; growth is tax-deferred.	**Tax:** See Limitations Imposed by Law.
	Loans: Limited to the lesser of $50,000 or ½ of the total account balance, including pre- and after-tax contributions, and all company matches, reduced by any outstanding loans. Must generally be repaid in 5 years, unless the loan is for the purchase of the principal residence. Getting a loan is not a taxable event. Interest is not deductible in most cases.	**Loans:** See Limitations Imposed by Law. Plan (or policy incorporated into the plan by reference) must set out rules governing loans.
	Withdrawals: Permitted in 6 cases. In all cases, the withdrawal appears on IRS Form 1099-R, and is fully taxable unless rolled over into another tax-deferred account or paid out as a "life annuity." Early withdrawal tax penalty of 10% applies in cases indicated by (*), unless rolled over. 1) disability 2) reaching the age of 59½ 3) severance from the company after age 55 4) severance from the company before age 55 (*) 5) death 6) financial hardship (*)	**Withdrawals:** For hardship withdrawals, the plan must set forth objective standards for determining whether there is a heavy financial need and the amount necessary to satisfy that need. (Example: the purchase of a primary residence or the payment of medical expenses.)

	Limitations Imposed by Law	Limitations Imposed by the Plan
Pretax Employee Contributions Also called "Elective"	**Elective Maximum Contribution:** $9,500/ year.	**Elective Minimum-Maximum:** 1% to 18%+ of salary.
	Overall Maximum Contribution: All contributions (pretax, after-tax, company matches, and forfeitures), taken together, may not exceed the lesser of: (a) 25% of the employee's compensation or (b) $30,000.	**Overall Maximum:** See Limitations Imposed by Law.
	Maximum for Highly Compensated Employees: Generally, employees earning $66,000+ are limited to (a) 1.25 × non-HCE average or (b) 2 × non-HCE average but not more than 2% more.	**Maximum for Highly Compensated Employees:** See Limitations Imposed by Law.
	Vesting: 100% immediate vesting.	**Vesting:** 100% immediate vesting.
After-tax Employee Contributions Also called "Voluntary"	**Tax:** Contributions *are* included as income in W-2; growth is tax-deferred.	**Tax:** See Limitations Imposed by Law.
	Withdrawals: Because you have already paid income taxes on after-tax contributions, withdrawals will appear on IRS Form 1099-R as *nontaxable.* You owe no income tax at the time of the withdrawal and no early withdrawal tax penalties are payable, except on earnings withdrawn.	**Withdrawals:** See Limitations Imposed by Law. See also Company Match, below.
	Maximum: See Pretax Overall Max.	**Minimum-Maximum:** 0–10% of salary.

(continued)

	Limitations Imposed by Law	Limitations Imposed by the Plan
Company Contributions on Employee Pre-Tax or After-Tax Contributions Also called "Match"	**Vesting:** Plan may provide not longer than either (a) 100% vesting after 5 years or (b) 20%/year in the 3rd through 7th years.	**Vesting:** See Limitations Imposed by Law.
	Tax: Contributions are *not* included as income in W-2; growth is tax-deferred.	**Tax:** See Limitations Imposed by Law.
	Withdrawals: Only vested portions may be withdrawn. The 6 pretax withdrawal cases apply, with 1 additional: 7) to the extent permitted by the plan	**Withdrawals:** Plan may provide certain types of withdrawals. See Limitations Imposed by Law.
	Maximum: See Pretax Overall Max.	**Minimum-Maximum:** Plan design dictates. Range can be 0–200% up to 10% pretax contribution. Typically 50% on 6% pretax contribution. May also be a scale, for example: 25% on first 1% 50% on next 2% 75% on next 1% 100% on next 1%

4

The Three Most Important Decisions You Have to Make

Your 401(k) offers you the opportunity to become financially self-sufficient in retirement. Whether you achieve this goal depends on three decisions you control: (1) what you contribute, (2) how you invest, and (3) how you withdraw. Your job as a 401(k) investor is to understand how to make these decisions wisely.

DECISION 1: WHAT YOU CONTRIBUTE

You saw in Chapter 2 that Holly decided to contribute at a level that triggered the maximum company match (in dollars). By doing this she was able to almost triple her "investment" of $22.50 to $60.00, immediately, without any market risk.

Holly was able to do this by asking herself, **"What do I need to do to take full advantage of the immediate compounding elements of my plan?"** By looking at her plan this way, she found she needed to contribute 6 percent pretax. At 6 percent, she received the highest match in dollars and in percentage. At this level of pretax contribution, she was able to maximize the benefits her plan offered.

If she had asked herself how much she could spare from her paycheck, she might not have participated at all. By looking at this decision as an investment decision, she was able to leverage her

investment dollars for retirement to the fullest, without assuming
any risk.

DECISION 2: WHAT INVESTMENTS YOU SELECT

In selecting her investments, Holly asked herself, **"What do I
need to choose to reach my objective of building my retirement
asset base?"** Studies show that vast numbers of 401(k) participants
pick money market funds or their company stock as their favorite
holdings. In choosing investments, it is a mistake to ask yourself,
What can I pick that is "safe" or familiar? You will see why shortly.

   In Chapter 8, I will introduce the three investment phases of
the 401(k) as well as the risk/reward characteristics of various
investment options. Then you will be able to see why Holly chose
the growth fund and the stock index fund as her investment
options to reach her objective.

   By knowing the risk and reward characteristics of the selections
offered by her plan, Holly was able to choose assets that had the
best long-term accumulation characteristics. She positioned herself in the more volatile and potentially more rewarding investments during the accumulation phase of her plan. This is the
optimal strategy for someone in the early accumulation phase of
his or her 401(k).

DECISION 3: HOW TO WITHDRAW IN RETIREMENT

In withdrawing from her plan in retirement, Holly asked herself,
**"What do I need to do to maximize my after-tax income stream
during my retirement?"** In Chapter 2, we compared Holly's
possible income stream after (1) taking a lump sum distribution at
retirement and (2) staying in a tax-deferred account. If Holly had
liquidated her account when she retired, she would have lost a
large chunk of her retirement assets to taxes. Instead she waited a
few years to continue building her account, and then, at manda-

tory distribution time, she chose to get tax advice on how to lower her taxes while maintaining a high after-tax income stream. After paying taxes, she had a large check to pay herself every year. In addition, the amount of her check was large enough to cover the impact of inflation.

RULES YOU NEED TO LIVE BY AS A 401(K) PARTICIPANT

Don't make the mistake of checking a box on your enrollment form without understanding the consequences of your choice. Remember, how much you contribute is *not* a budget decision. How much you contribute is an investment decision. To put things in perspective, ask yourself the following questions.

1. Do I want to get more for my investment dollar by investing in my 401(k) instead of a regular account?
2. Do I want to leverage my paycheck to increase my investment without putting up more money?
3. Do I want a special bonus from my company for participating in the plan?
4. Do I want to leverage my company match to get more 401(k) dollars than I would with a regular bonus?
5. Do I want to grow my investments on a tax-deferred basis?
6. Do I want to grow my account by reinvesting my account earnings?

By asking these questions and maintaining the perspective of an investor, you will discover the correct course to take in your particular situation.

Next ask yourself, **"What do I need to do to take full advantage of the immediate compounding elements of my plan?"** Asking this question will lead you to the optimal level of contribution you need to make to maximize the dollar benefit of your plan. In the next chapter, I will take you through an analysis of your plan so that you will be able to determine the best contribution level for yourself.

Then ask yourself, **"What investment do I need to choose in order to reach my objective of building my retirement asset base?"** The size of your retirement asset base needs to be large enough to cover inflation and taxes. In Chapters 6, 7, 8, and 9, I will take you through an investment analysis so that you can determine the best place to be in terms of investment selections as you go through the different phases of your 401(k).

When you are ready to retire, you will ask yourself, **"What do I need to do to maximize my after-tax income stream?"** This question will lead you to explore the investment and tax effects of your various options and to choose the optimal methodology for keeping your taxes low and your income stream as high as possible. In Chapter 10, I will help you understand the issues underlying retirement withdrawals.

YOUR STRATEGY

Holly had a game plan. She knew what she wanted her 401(k) to do for her. That is, she wanted to create a retirement asset base large enough to pay her a satisfactory after-tax income stream in retirement. This was the 401(k) objective she set for herself.

She wanted the most help she could get from her plan in order to accomplish this result, so she figured out her maximum leverage points. To keep things in perspective, she also decided early that she would not withdraw money until she needed it at retirement, and that she would not borrow against her account. She also decided up front that if she were to change jobs, she would not cash out her 401(k), pay taxes and penalties on the distribution, and spend the remainder. This game plan gave Holly every chance for making the most of her 401(k), with the least hardship. In fact, because of payroll deductions, she never even missed the money she was contributing.

In determining your own game plan, remember that the

amount you contribute and how you invest will drive your 401(k) results. You will see immediate results from your contribution decisions and you will see long-term results from your investment decisions. Each supports the other. Both are essential to meeting your 401(k) objective of creating a sufficient income stream for yourself in retirement.

Because the first two decisions drive the compounding factors, it is of utmost importance that you understand how your choices will play out over the years. This requires an understanding of the elements of your 401(k) and the consequences of each of your options.

The next few chapters will help you arrive at good contribution and investment decisions. As you read them, start to think in terms of the objectives you would like to establish for your own 401(k). In addition, start to think about the other elements of your game plan. What will you do to reach your objectives? What investment can help you achieve the results you are looking for? How much should you contribute? Will you borrow from your 401(k) if you need to buy a new car? If you change jobs, will you cash out your 401(k) and spend the money?

In addition, think about how you will monitor your progress and how you will know if you are on course. How often will you review your account? What will you be looking for?

5

How to Maximize
Immediate Compounding

One of the decisions you will be called upon to make as a 401(k) participant is *deceptively* simple: When and how much should I contribute to the plan?

Beneath the surface of this very basic decision lies the single most important driver of your results, particularly if your plan provides a company match. That is, among other things, what you decide to contribute affects what your company contributes, sometimes directly, sometimes indirectly. *This is why you must understand the ramifications of this and other choices you are called upon to make in your plan, even if they appear to be the most basic of decisions driven by your* budget.

If you are currently a participant, you need to revisit your contributions now to ensure that you are maximizing your 401(k). Here is what you need to do. After you read this chapter, get the answers to *all* of the following contribution questions. (You'll fill in the answers in the the contribution questionnaire at the end of this chapter.) Do not skip any question and *hold off on budgetary concerns until you find out the answers.* You will see how your answers will affect your decisions, shortly. After you complete the contribution questionnaire, you will be able to fill in the Immediate 401(k) Benefits Table at the end of this chapter, which will help you determine how to maximize your immediate compounding benefits.

Contribution Questions

1. What are the minimum and maximum amounts I may contribute pretax?
2. What are the minimum and maximum amounts I may contribute after-tax?
3. Is there a company match or contribution, and if so, how does it work? Ask the same question about any possible profit sharing that might be tied to the plan, or any other way in which the company pays into the plan for your benefit.
4. How much do I need to contribute to maximize the company match (or other company contribution)?

Your primary resource will be your human resources, personnel, or benefits officer. He or she will be able to answer questions 1, 2, and 3 and give you a booklet that summarizes the features of your plan in writing. In some cases, question 4, which you must answer before you proceed, may require you to read the summary plan description.

As you read through the rest of this chapter, think of your employee pretax (and after-tax) contribution to the plan as the amount you pay to purchase an investment. As you consider the examples, think of the return you get by operation of the plan at different levels of contribution. Look for ways to maximize this investment and consider the risks associated with your options. Notice that we are not discussing investment options here, only how much you should contribute to the plan, based on the plan itself and the advantages it offers participants.

To give you an example of what you might find in your plan, let's look at the plan offered by a midsize northeastern company employing 10,000 people. If you go to the benefits director and ask about the 401(k), you will receive information about the company's employee savings and stock ownership plan. You will find out that you are eligible to participate in the plan if you work full-time and have been with the company for one year.

Now, you want to know how to take maximum advantage of the

plan, so you ask our four questions, one at a time, and record your answers in the questionnaire provided at the end of this chapter. The first two questions are very easy, but start to notice some of the ramifications.

1. What are the minimum and maximum amounts I may contribute pretax?

In our example, you find that you can contribute not less than 1 percent nor more than 18 percent of your pay in "before and after-tax contributions." For someone making $50,000 that would mean a maximum contribution of $9,000 (18 percent) and a minimum of $500 a year (1 percent). This information will give you the outside limits of what you can contribute.

Looking at this information as an investor, remember the compounding elements discussed in Chapter 2?

Question: What ramifications do you see, not knowing anything else about the plan at this point?

Answer: Pretax contributions give you immediate and long-term compounding potential, by setting into motion four compounding elements, the Pretax Advantage, Leveraged Paycheck, Tax-Deferred Growth, and Reinvestment Privilege. After-tax contributions offer only the last two.

Question: If you contribute 18 percent, how much is going into your plan each year? How much is coming out of your paycheck? And, what are your year-end tax savings?

Answer: While $9,000 is going into your plan, only $6,750 is coming out of your paycheck, because of tax adjustments assuming a 25 percent tax rate. In addition, you save $2,250 in taxes at tax time, just because you are participating in the plan. Your investment is $9,000 but your out-of-pocket cost is $6,750.

Question: If you contribute 1 percent, how much is going into your plan each year? How much is coming out of your paycheck? And what are your year-end tax savings?

Answer: While $500 is going into your plan, only $375 is coming out of your paycheck, because of tax adjustments assuming a 25 percent tax rate. In addition, you save $125 in taxes at tax time, just because you are participating in the plan. Your investment is $500, but your out-of-pocket cost is only $375.

2. What are the minimum and maximum amounts I may contribute after-tax?

The minimum is zero, since there is no requirement to contribute after-tax. The maximum depends on how much you are contributing to your pretax account and plan limits. Because tax benefits are greater in your pretax account, you should use all of your pretax allocations before using any after-tax allocations. In our example, if you contribute all of your 18 percent maximum contribution to pretax, your maximum after-tax contribution will be zero.

3. Is there a company match or contribution, and if so, how does it work?

It is very important to understand how the company match (or profit-sharing or other company contributions) works in your plan. (If your plan does not offer a company match, please skip to page 73.) Your match supports two compounding elements, immediately compounding your own investment in the amount of the match, and giving you leverage by deferring the tax that would normally be due on this company "bonus." In addition, the match puts into motion the fifth and sixth compounding elements.

In our example, you find that your company matches your pre- and after-tax contributions 100 percent, up to a maximum of 6 percent of your salary. This means that for every dollar you contribute, your company contributes one dollar to your 401(k) account. If you contribute $500, your company will contribute $500. If you contribute $1,000, your company will contribute $1,000.

Are you thinking in terms of "return" on your "investment" when you have a company match? I will come back to this question, shortly.

At the compensation level in our example, there is no other limitation on the maximum contributions. I will look at higher compensation levels in Chapter 12, to see how the tax laws affect maximum company matches.

You also want to know if your match is paid in cash, company stock, or some other form and when it is paid. If your match is paid in company stock, you have to be certain to diversify your overall 401(k) holdings, to lower the risk of your overall portfolio. I touch on diversification again in Chapters 6 and 13.

4. How much do I need to contribute to maximize the company match (or other company contribution)?

There is no requirement for a company to offer a match. Those that do want to help you save. If you work for a firm that does offer a matching contribution, you are in an enviable position. Because matches are usually tied to a percentage of your contribution up to a certain percentage of salary, you have to figure out how much to contribute in order to get the maximum benefit from the match.

In our example, the match is 100 percent of your contribution, with a cap at 6 percent of salary. Some of you may say that any percentage up to and including 6 percent constitutes the maximum, since you are being matched 100 percent at any of those levels.

What you are missing is the dollar amount into which the percentage contribution will translate.

Look at a 1 percent contribution. What is the dollar benefit of the match for a 1 percent contribution on your part?

Answer: $500. Your company's 100 percent match translates into $500. The percentage benefit of your match is 100 percent and the dollar benefit of your match is $500.

Compare a 6 percent match. What is the dollar benefit of the match for a 6 percent contribution on your part?

Answer: $3,000. The percentage benefit of your match is 100 percent and the dollar benefit of your match is $3,000 (6 percent of $50,000).

So you can see that in one case, your company match is $500, and in the other, your company match is $3,000. What does this tell you? You cannot consider the percentage alone; you also need to consider the dollar amount into which the percentage translates in your particular case.

With the optimal use of the match, you are in effect paying yourself a special bonus, which is available to anyone who spends a minimal amount of time doing a little research about his or her plan. To emphasize the benefit of the match, remember that matches offer two compounding elements, the bonus itself and immediate tax deferral of the bonus; in addition, the match drives two more compounding elements, Tax Deferred Growth and Reinvestment Privilege.

It is of utmost importance to understand your match and the leverage it offers in dollars, not percentages. When you are looking for the answer to question 4, be sure you understand *both* the percentage contribution and the dollar contribution that your company will be making, and how to maximize both. Of the four questions, you can see that the fourth may be the most important.

There are additional points you need to consider.

What is the investment return on the company match?
Have you thought of the match in terms of how it affects your return on your initial "investment"—your contribution?

Question: Have you noticed that your return is over 100 percent? What risk did you have to take to double your money so quickly?

Answer: You did not have to take any investment risk in order to more than double your money. At the 6 percent contribution level you invested $2,250 (paycheck reduction). However, $3,000 was placed into your account on your behalf as your contribution and another $3,000 was placed into your company match account by your company. The match is yours to keep as soon as it vests.

There is no single alternative available to you as an investor that immediately doubles your money—guaranteed—without risk. That is, with a dollar-for-dollar match, every single dollar you are "putting into" your 401(k) up to 6 percent of your salary is immediately doubling. However, you are getting the largest dollar amount contribution from the company at the 6 percent level. If you decided to contribute anything less than 6 percent of your salary, you gave up money the company was willing to give you as a bonus in your company match account. In this plan, 6 percent is the best place to position yourself as a 401(k) investor. You are getting the maximum dollar benefit out of the company match.

If you do your homework, you can find the maximum benefit of your 401(k) that will automatically boost your investment earnings by the maximum company match. In plans with a 100 percent match, you can double your money instantaneously. In more generous plans, offering 200 percent matching, you can triple your money instantaneously.

There is a wide range of possibilities for company matches. A large number of companies determine their match based on a fixed percentage of salary, as in the above example. Those plans make it easy to identify your best position. Other plans may not have a match at all. Still others may tie the match to the performance of the company.

If your 401(k) company contribution is tied to profits, your "match" will depend on how the company is doing. For example, in one plan, in order for there to be a contribution, the company has to make a return on assets of at least 8.5 percent. At that level, a flat $100 is paid by the company to each employee. If the company's return on assets is 12 percent, then the company's contribution is 3.5 percent of your pay, no matter how much you contribute. If the return on assets is 16.5 percent, then the contribution is 10 percent of your pay.

This will illustrate how this type of profit-sharing contribution would work if you contribute a minimum of 1 percent, assuming a return on assets of 12 percent. At a 12 percent return on assets, the company contributes 3.5 percent of your pay or $1,750 (3.5 percent of $50,000) no matter how much you contribute. If you contribute 1 percent or $500 your company will contribute $1,750. If you contribute 6 percent or $3,000, your company will still contribute $1,750.

With a 401(k) profit-sharing plan that does not also have a company match, you can see that your contribution will not affect the company's contributions, regardless of the amount of the company's profit sharing.

If your plan does not provide a company match:
Many 401(k) plans provide some sort of company match or contribution. If yours does not, you will not get as much leverage out of your 401(k) as you would if it did. However, that is no reason not to participate in the plan.

In your case, you should think of your 401(k) as a supercharged IRA, in which the government is lending you money to invest. You still get the benefits of the Pretax Advantage, Leveraged Paycheck, Tax-Deferred Growth, and the Reinvestment Privilege. No other investment can give you these benefits.

How can I manage to contribute without lowering my paycheck more than I can afford?
After you have found the best place to be in terms of your optimal contribution, you will need to find out if you can afford to make the contribution. Remember that your percentage "salary reduction" is not the same as the percentage actually taken from your paycheck to fund the contribution. This is due to adjustments that are made for taxes, as we saw in Chapter 2.

As in the example shown on page 68 of this chapter, the salary reduction of $9,000 that was used as an employee contribution did not reduce the paycheck by the full $9,000, but only by $6,750, because of tax adjustments. In Chapter 2, Holly's salary reduction of $30 per week, which was used as an employee contribution, did not reduce her paycheck by $30, but only by $22.50, due to tax adjustments.

When you are considering budgetary constraints, you must be sure to understand the dollar amount that comes out of your paycheck and weigh that against the value of your contribution in terms of 401(k) benefits you are acquiring. Only then are you in a position to judge whether you can afford to make a larger contribution to your plan. Usually, you will find you can't afford not to increase your contribution to maximize your company contribution.

In some cases, comparing these numbers alone will help you decide what to do. In other cases, where the amounts deducted from your paycheck appear too high for you to live with, talk to your payroll department about the effect of adjusting your withholding to account for the tax savings you will reap at the time you file your tax return. Any withholding adjustments should be done carefully, with tax advice, so that at the end of the year, you not find yourself owing the IRS money you do not have.

With careful management of your withholding, you can keep your paycheck as high as possible and maximize your 401(k) at the same time.

The following questionnaire and tables will help you pull all this information together, so that you will know how much to contribute to your plan, the maximum effect in terms of the plan, and the tax effect of different contribution levels.

As you go about finding out the answers to these questions, you will need to find the best source of information in your company.

There are three sources of information available to you: (1) your human resources department, (2) your 401(k) administrator, and (3) your investment managers. In some companies, the 401(k) function is outsourced and you will need to deal with someone by phone. In any event, the place to start is your human resources department.

CONTRIBUTION QUESTIONNAIRE

Decision 1: How Much Should I Contribute?

1. What are the minimum and maximum amounts I may contribute pretax?

   - *Minimum in percent:* ____%
   - *Minimum in dollars:* $____*per year and* $____*per paycheck*
   - *Maximum in percent:* ____%
   - *Maximum in dollars:* $____*per year and* $____*per paycheck*

2. What are the minimum and maximum amounts I may contribute after-tax?

   - *Minimum in percent:* ____%
   - *Minimum in dollars:* $____*per year and* $____*per paycheck*
   - *Maximum in percent:* ____%
   - *Maximum in dollars:* $____*per year and* $____*per paycheck*

3. Is there a company match or contribution, and if so, how does it work?

   - *Is there a company contribution?*
     YES ____NO ____ If NO, skip to question 6.
   - *If YES, does it depend on how much I contribute?*
     YES ____NO ____
   - *If YES, is there a cap on the match that is tied to my contributions?*
     YES ____NO ____
   - *If YES, what is the cap?* ____
   - *What is the minimum I need to contribute for:*

a) the maximum percentage company match? $ ____
b) the maximum dollar company match? $ ____

4. How much do I need to contribute to maximize the company match (or other company contribution)?

■ *What do I need to contribute to earn the maximum dollar contribution from the company? $ ____*
■ *At the contribution levels for which I can maximize the company match, what is the amount by which my paycheck will be reduced? $ ____*
■ *At that level, how much will my contribution buy me in terms of immediate 401(k) benefits, not considering investments? $ ____*
■ *What will I have left in my paycheck compared to now? $ ____*

5. Will the maximum limits imposed by the tax laws affect me?

■ *Is my maximum pretax contribution going to be limited by the tax laws? If so, what is the maximum I may contribute pretax? $ ____ per year*
■ *Is my maximum after-tax contribution going to be limited by the tax laws? If so, what is the maximum I may contribute after-tax? $ ____ per year*

6. How can I manage to contribute without lowering my paycheck more than I can afford?

■ *How much is currently being withheld for tax purposes? $ ____*
■ *If I increase my pretax contribution, how much should I adjust withholding to increase my paycheck? $ ____*
■ *Can I increase my contribution to the maximum leverage point under my plan and adjust my withholding in such a way as to cover my taxes at tax time through withholding if desirable? YES ____ NO ____*

Putting It All Together

The answers to questions 1 through 4 will help you figure out how much you need to contribute to maximize your plan. You need to know that number and the effect of taxes on your paycheck if you want to adjust your withholding to keep your paycheck as high as possible, while making sure your taxes are covered.

Only after you have done these calculations, and answered questions 5 and 6 with the help of your human resources department, are you in a position to decide how much you should contribute pretax. As you can see, your budget is not a concern until you know how much Uncle Sam is willing to forgo in income taxes on your earnings to encourage you to save in your 401(k). If you do have a budgetary issue, make certain you understand what your paycheck adjustment will "buy" for you in 401(k) benefits. Remember that this is one case in which it pays to pay yourself first.

After you have the answers to these questions, you might wish to complete the following Immediate 401(k) Benefits table to find the maximum leverage points of your plan. Filled-in tables at different contribution levels are provided as examples.

By completing this table, you will see how to maximize immediate compounding in your particular case. You will need to have your effective tax rate from page 43 and the answers to the contribution questionnaire beginning on page 75. After completing the table you will be ready to turn to investment decisions, which are covered in Chapters 6 through 9.

IMMEDIATE 401(K) BENEFITS
1% Contribution Example
Showing effect of payroll deduction, tax benefits, and
company contribution (match or profit sharing)

Enter % You Are Considering

% of Salary You Are Considering Contributing	1.00%

Enter Your Assumptions

Effective Tax Rate (Fed + St)	33.00%
Annual Compensation	$50,000
Match (or Profit-Sharing Contribution)	50.00%
Company Match Caps Out Where?	6.00%

Your Paychecks Before Enrollment in the Plan

Annual Compensation	$50,000
Tax	$16,500
Paycheck Before Enrollment	$33,500

Contributions

Your Contribution	$500
Company Match	$250
Your Contribution + Company Match	$750

Your Paychecks After Enrollment

Annual Compensation	$50,000
Your Contribution	$500
Adjusted Salary (Salary − Your Contribution)	$49,500
Adjusted Tax	$16,335
Paycheck After Enrollment	$33,165

The "Cost of Your Investment"

Difference in Paychecks (Before and After Enrollment)	$335

Benefit of Participating, Considering Immediate Compounding

From the IRS (Effect of Adjusted Tax)	$165
From the Company (Match or Profit Sharing)	$250
From Your Paycheck	$335
Value of Your Account After Enrolling	$750
Immediate Benefit of Enrollment	$415

IMMEDIATE 401(K) BENEFITS
6% Contribution Example
Showing effect of payroll deduction, tax benefits, and
company contribution (match or profit sharing)

Enter % You Are Considering	
% of Salary You Are Considering Contributing	6.00%
Enter Your Assumptions	
Effective Tax Rate (Fed + St)	33.00%
Annual Compensation	$50,000
Match (or Profit-Sharing Contribution)	50.00%
Company Match Caps Out Where?	6.00%
Your Paychecks Before Enrollment in the Plan	
Annual Compensation	$50,000
Tax	$16,500
Paycheck Before Enrollment	$33,500
Contributions	
Your Contribution	$3,000
Company Match	$1,500
Your Contribution + Company Match	$4,500
Your Paychecks After Enrollment	
Annual Compensation	$50,000
Your Contribution	$3,000
Adjusted Salary (Salary − Your Contribution)	$47,000
Adjusted Tax	$15,510
Paycheck After Enrollment	$31,490
The "Cost of Your Investment"	
Difference in Paychecks (Before and After Enrollment)	$2,010
Benefit of Participating, Considering Immediate Compounding	
From the IRS (Effect of Adjusted Tax)	$990
From the Company (Match or Profit Sharing)	$1,500
From Your Paycheck	$2,010
Value of Your Account After Enrolling	$4,500
Immediate Benefit of Enrollment	$2,490

IMMEDIATE 401(K) BENEFITS
9% Contribution Example
Showing effect of payroll deduction, tax benefits, and
company contribution (match or profit sharing)

Enter % You Are Considering

% of Salary You Are Considering Contributing	9.00%

Enter Your Assumptions

Effective Tax Rate (Fed + St)	33.00%
Annual Compensation	$50,000
Match (or Profit-Sharing Contribution)	50.00%
Company Match Caps Out Where?	6.00%

Your Paychecks Before Enrollment in the Plan

Annual Compensation	$50,000
Tax	$16,500
Paycheck Before Enrollment	$33,500

Contributions

Your Contribution	$4,500
Company Match	$1,500
Your Contribution + Company Match	$6,000

Your Paychecks After Enrollment

Annual Compensation	$50,000
Your Contribution	$4,500
Adjusted Salary (Salary − Your Contribution)	$45,500
Adjusted Tax	$15,015
Paycheck After Enrollment	$30,485

The "Cost of Your Investment"

Difference in Paychecks (Before and After Enrollment)	$3,015

Benefit of Participating, Considering Immediate Compounding

From the IRS (Effect of Adjusted Tax)	$1,485
From the Company (Match or Profit Sharing)	$1,500
From Your Paycheck	$3,015
Value of Your Account After Enrolling	$6,000
Immediate Benefit of Enrollment	$2,985

IMMEDIATE 401(K) BENEFITS
Blank Table to Fill In

Showing effect of payroll deduction, tax benefits, and company contribution (match or profit sharing). Enter your assumptions, then make a copy: Use a different copy of this form for each % contribution you are considering.

Enter % You Are Considering
% of Salary You Are Considering Contributing ☐

Enter Your Assumptions
Effective Tax Rate (Fed + St) ☐
Annual Compensation ☐
Match (or Profit-Sharing Contribution) ☐
Company Match Caps Out Where? ☐

Your Paychecks Before Enrollment in the Plan
Annual Compensation ☐
Tax ☐
Paycheck Before Enrollment ☐

Contributions
Your Contribution ☐
Company Match ☐
Your Contribution + Company Match ☐

Your Paychecks After Enrollment
Annual Compensation ☐
Your Contribution ☐
Adjusted Salary (Salary − Your Contribution) ☐
Adjusted Tax ☐
Paycheck After Enrollment ☐

The "Cost of Your Investment"
Difference in Paychecks (Before and After Enrollment) ☐

Benefit of Participating, Considering Immediate Compounding
From the IRS (Effect of Adjusted Tax) ☐
From the Company (Match or Profit Sharing) ☐
From Your Paycheck ☐
Value of Your Account After Enrolling ☐
Immediate Benefit of Enrollment ☐

6

Understanding and Managing Risk

As a 401(k) investor, you have the opportunity to create an income stream for yourself in retirement. The amount of income you have will depend on three things: your contributions, your investments, and your withdrawals. I discussed contribution decisions in Chapter 5. Now let's turn to risks and investment decisions. First, in this chapter and the next, I will give you some insight into the risks of various investments you might use in your 401(k). Then I will show you how to put risk management principles to work for you in your 401(k).

Next to not participating in your company's 401(k) plan, an unreasonable fear of risk can be the single greatest reason you don't accumulate sufficient wealth over your working life to provide a comfortable retirement. As you read through the following discussion of risk, notice that risk and safety are relative concepts that depend on what you are trying to achieve. While you cannot control the markets, the extent to which your 401(k) investments are safe — or exposed to risk — is within your control.

The investment risk most people think of is short-term stock market loss. But there are a number of other identifiable risks associated with investing that can cause you to fail to meet your 401(k) objectives. They are: Market Risk, Credit Risk, Skill Risk, Inflation Risk, Tax Risk, and Adviser Risk.

Market Risk. Market risk is the risk that is associated with the financial market in which you are investing. Short-term market risk in the stock, bond, and commodity markets is very high. Long-term results in the stock and bond markets are more predictable. If you own government bonds, they will move in price with other government bonds of the same maturity. If you own a mutual fund that is diversified in such a way as to replicate the S&P 500 Index, your fund will move up and down with the market. The S&P 500 Index is a listing of 500 stocks compiled by Standard & Poor's to assess the overall U.S. stock market or "broad market." The Wilshire 5000 is another index of the broad market.

A diversified small capitalization fund will tend to move with the more volatile small-stock markets if the fund is true to its objectives. The Russell 2000 Index is used as a measure of the small-stock market, composed of 2,000 stocks of companies that are small in capitalization.

The risk of money market funds is not risk of loss of principal, since money market funds are priced at a stable one dollar per share. The market risk inherent in money market funds is a return risk. Interest rates for money markets reflect the market for short-term borrowing rates, which vary significantly reflecting demand for money and inflation. Money market returns in the last 15 years have varied from 3 percent to a short period in the late 1970s and early 1980s when returns were in the double digits. We will discuss money market funds again under Inflation Risk.

Market risk is a very acceptable risk for an investor to assume. There is a great deal of information about how U.S.[1] financial markets act over the long or short term. Given the extent of information available about good and bad markets, crashes, periods of high inflation, and wide swings in interest rates, there should be no surprises to the informed investor as to possible market movements. The future will be some variation of the past.

To give you an example of what you might expect, let's go back

---

[1] The currency exchange risk inherent in investing overseas is an added risk that is not inherent in U.S. stock and bond markets.

to 1967, when you begin investing $100 per month in an S&P
Index fund. By September 1987, you have invested $24,000, and
your account is valued at about $116,000. Next month, your
account drops along with the market crash of October 1987. By
the end of the month, your account is down $25,000. That
certainly gets your attention, especially in the context of news-
paper headlines recalling the great stock market crash of 1929.

How you react will depend on your purpose for buying the index
fund. If you are in the middle stages of accumulating assets for
retirement, you need not liquidate your holdings and lock in your
losses. Your strategy might be to continue to acquire shares, which
are now available at much more favorable prices. If you continue
investing $100 per month, by September 1995 you have invested a
total of $33,000, but your account is now worth over $275,000.

On the other hand, if you bought the index fund in anticipation
of a lump-sum withdrawal at the end of 1987, and this fund is your
only holding, you are out of luck. You simply do not have enough
time to make use of the buying opportunity and you will be forced
to sell shares at a loss to cover your withdrawal. You pay the
penalty for lack of diversification and failure to appreciate short-
term price volatility.

If you want to look for reasons not to be in the stock market,
you'll find them. On the other hand, if you understand that
markets involve the risk of price movements, you will be able to
participate wisely.

Credit Risk. Credit risk is an issue when you invest in an
individual company's stocks or bonds. Credit risk encompasses
the market share the company has for its products, competition
from domestic and foreign companies in the same business, inept
management, changes in technology, and any other good or bad
events in the company's life that are reflected in the price of its
stocks and bonds.

The stocks of the Dow Jones Industrial Average provide good
examples of the reflection of credit risk in stock prices. Merck,
McDonald's, and Coca-Cola were star performers during 1980–
95, in contrast to Bethlehem Steel and Woolworth. If you had

invested in Merck, McDonald's, or Coca-Cola, you would have handsomely outperformed the Dow Jones Average. Had you chosen Bethlehem Steel or Woolworth you would have had a performance record that was less than stellar.

Credit risk in your 401(k) extends to your investment in your employer's stock. Your company stock is a nondiversified position that reflects the management and fortunes of the company and will be more volatile than a diversified portfolio. In cases in which your 401(k) pays a company match or profit-sharing contribution in shares of company stock, you will need to be particularly aware of the need to diversify your employee contribution accounts and other holdings to reduce the risk of concentration.

Skill (Decision) Risk. Some people are good athletes and others are klutzes. Some people are good traders and others just don't have the talent. If you think you can profitably trade your 401(k) by moving into and out of different investment selections, you may incur significant losses before you realize you don't have the skill to make money consistently over long periods of time. There is little evidence that attempting to anticipate market moves is more profitable over the long term than holding while reinvesting earnings. The most profitable approach for most 401(k) investors is to make an appropriate initial decision and have the patience, knowledge, and fortitude to stay the course. You make more money by participating in the markets than by trading.

Inflation Risk. Inflation is a risk to 401(k) investors only if they stick to money market funds or short-term fixed-income instruments for the long term. Historically, with the exception of a few years in the late 1970s and early 1980s, there is little profit left over in money markets and short-term fixed-income investments after the effect of inflation — not sufficient in amount to make these instruments viable investment options for your 401(k). When balancing the risk/reward tradeoffs of an investment option for your 401(k), remember that stability of principal has its price. In the case of money market funds and short-term fixed-income instruments, the benefits of stability of principal are outweighed by the limited returns these instruments offer after inflation.

Tax Risk. Taxes are not a risk to the 401(k) investor during accumulation, but they are if you are considering taking a loan or withdrawing funds. Managing your withdrawals and loans correctly will protect you from the risk of loss due to taxes.

Adviser Risk. Adviser risk is the risk of bad advice. Your company has screened the investment managers of the funds that have been selected for your plan. You can reasonably rely on your company's assessment. Your company should continue to monitor the performance of the funds to determine that there is continuing good management.

You might be tempted to turn to your human resources department, your boss, or friends for guidance on how to invest your 401(k). If you do, you are exposing yourself to adviser risk. Likewise, if you make decisions based on fund rankings or market or fund commentary in newsletters or advisory publications about fund selection or switching, you are exposed to adviser risk.

To put this mosaic of risks into perspective in your situation, you need to understand where you are going with your 401(k). *That is, you need to keep in mind that your overriding purpose in participating in your 401(k) is to ensure a satisfactory income stream in retirement. In order to do that, you need to focus on building your assets while you are working. During this period of time, the safety you are seeking as a 401(k) investor is not the safety offered by stability of principal over the short term. It is the security of knowing that you are on a course that will help you accumulate assets to secure your future. The risk you have to worry about is the risk of doing something that will prevent you from building those retirement assets and creating that retirement income stream.*

In the next chapter, I will take a closer look at your risk/reward tradeoffs.

7

Making the Markets Work for You

Why do people put their money at risk in the financial markets? Why don't they just pick stable price investments like the money market fund or a guaranteed investment contract to protect their principal? The answer lies in fully understanding the risk/reward dynamic of the markets. As you saw in Chapter 6, an investment with a stable value may avoid the risk of fluctuation of principal, but it does not avoid the risk of inflation. That is, the price for stability of principal is no real return after inflation. Consequently, these instruments will not be very useful in terms of building your 401(k) assets.

Individuals who purchase investments that fluctuate in price, such as stocks, bonds, and mutual funds, are less concerned with fluctuation of principal over the short term and more concerned with getting the long-term returns they need to build their retirement capital. The tradeoff for fluctuation is the potential for return, and that is the potential payoff and the reason why people are willing to put their money at risk in the financial markets.

In this chapter, I will look at risk more closely, so you can become more comfortable with what you can expect from your investments. As you will see, your success in building adequate retirement capital will depend on your understanding and managing the risk/reward relationship. The essential elements to understand and manage are: price movements of the financial instruments in which you invest, your holding period, and how you use any income produced by the investment during your holding period. As you read through the discussion that follows, pay attention to these elements and think about how you would manage them. Try to come up with a reasonable set of rules that you would use to manage your 401(k) from now through retirement.

Since many of your 401(k) choices will involve mutual funds investing in stocks, and possibly your company stock, let's look at the stock market and compare different asset classes. An asset class is a particular kind of investment, such as treasury bills, long-term government bonds, gold, large-capitalization stocks, small-capitalization stocks, and any other group of investments or commodities that can be bought or sold on a market.

I will limit the discussion of stocks to two major asset classes: New York Stock Exchange (NYSE) listed stocks issued by large companies and NYSE listed stocks issued by small companies. If all the stocks listed in the NYSE were ranked by capitalization from largest to smallest and grouped into 10 rankings, the top four rankings would be the large companies. The bottom two rankings would be the small stocks. When I discuss the broad stock market, I am referring to large company stocks represented by Standard and Poor's Index of 500 stocks (S&P). The bottom 9th and 10th rankings of the NYSE listed stocks represent the small-stock market.[1]

Understanding the comparative price characteristics of these two asset classes will give you a basis for judging some of the stock mutual funds that will be available for you to select for your 401(k).

The stock market is a place in which investors can make money by buying a stock at one price and selling the stock to another investor at a higher price. Implicit in every stock purchase is the anticipation of a profit on its sale as well as the probability of a loss in the event of a sale at a lower price.

There is far greater risk in investing in a single stock than in a

[1] *Stocks, Bonds, Bills, and Inflation 1996 Yearbook*™, Ibbotson Associates, Chicago (annually updates work by Roger G. Ibbotson and Rex A. Sinquefield). Used with permission. All rights reserved.

diversified portfolio of stocks. A single stock has a risk called credit risk, which is the risk of the underlying company not faring well, or the market for its products changing before the company can adapt, or worse, the company failing. To avoid the risks and higher volatility of holding a single stock, investors diversify their portfolios among 15 or more stocks to adjust their risk to what is called "market risk."

Market risk is the risk associated with the broad market, small stocks, midsize stocks, or whichever market segment the portfolio is designed to participate in. Mutual funds are diversified portfolios of stocks with specified investment objectives that can offer risks ranging from very conservative to extremely aggressive. All other things being equal, the risks are greater for funds that invest in low-priced stocks. Of the six risks identified in Chapter 6, the risks involved here are the risks of loss of principal due to both credit risk and market risk.

In assessing changes in the S&P you would find that yearly returns are both negative and positive. That is, one year, the market might be down 20 percent and another year, it might be up 30 percent. One of your investment options in your 401(k) could be a stock index fund. If you bought an S&P Index fund in the beginning of the 30 percent up year, you would have made 30 percent if you sold your shares at the end of the year. If you bought the fund in the beginning of the 20 percent down year, you would have lost 20 percent if you sold the shares at the end of that year.

This price action is what is meant by volatility. That is, volatility is a measure of movement in the price of a stock or investment. Volatility can be measured at different intervals. We will be looking at year-to-year changes for purposes of our discussion. Although price movements can occur minute to minute in the stock market, mutual funds are typically priced once a day, usually as of the close of business on the New York Stock Exchange.

No matter how good the markets might appear to be at any particular time, by their very nature, the markets and the individual stocks composing the markets do *not* go up in price all the time. No one can guarantee that they will. The only guarantee anyone can give you is that stock prices will go up some of the time and down some of the time. Over the long term, the bias of the stock market is upward. The best way to get a true understanding of price action of the asset class you are considering is to look at price movement over different market periods, including the most volatile period.

THE MOST VOLATILE PERIOD IN THE STOCK MARKET

If you look at the 70-year period (1926–95) for which reliable stock market data is available, up years in the broad market outnumber down years more than two to one. From 1926 through 1995, there were 50 up years and 20 down years. As you might expect, most (almost half) of the down years occurred during the Depression and the years immediately following. These 12 years (1927–38) were the most *volatile* years in the stock market, representing the largest losses and greatest investment opportunities of the modern-day market.

During this period of time, the greatest loss year in the broad market was −43 percent (1931) and the greatest gain +54 percent (1933). These two years show the largest year-to-year fluctuations recorded during the 1926–95 period. Year-to-year fluctuations range between these two numbers—down 43 percent to up 54 percent—setting the outer limits of year-to-year returns in the market from 1926 to date. You need to be aware of these loss periods because the press will remind you of them the next time the market corrects itself in a significant manner. All the returns we have seen since 1938 fall within a more narrow range, from down 26.5 percent to up 53 percent.

In comparison, the small-stock market was much more volatile. The broadest range was between −58 percent and +143 percent. Four of the worst years were between −38 percent and −58 percent, all occurring between 1926 and 1938. Between 1939 and 1995, the range fell between −31 percent and +88 percent.

All of these returns show you volatility year over year. As we saw in Chapter 6, you could have a very short-interim fall in the market that will affect your account if you sell into that market and lock in your loss. Most of you will be able to hold for longer periods than a month or a year. In fact, you could potentially be investing in your 401(k) for your entire working career and you could be managing your 401(k) investments for another 30 years into your retirement. Based on what you have seen so far, consider how a longer holding period would affect your returns. As you read about Treasury bills and government bonds below, think what you consider safe and what you consider risky.

TREASURY BILL AND BOND RISKS AND REWARDS

If you examine another major asset class, U.S. Treasury bills, prices did not move during the period 1926–95, but interest payments did. Treasury bills are an example of a major asset class that has virtually no price volatility. Mutual funds that invest primarily in short-term U.S. Treasuries maturing in less than one year typically have prices per share figured at a stable one dollar per share and normally experience no volatility in price.

Government bonds are "safe" investments in terms of safety of principal and an income stream that is guaranteed by the U.S. government. Does that mean there is no risk in bonds? No. Government bonds are safe only if you don't need to sell them before maturity. If you do have to offer them for sale, you expose your bonds to market risk. You can keep them protected from market risk by holding them to maturity, but inflation risk could hurt your ending value.

But what happens if you have to sell? If you have to sell the bond before maturity you have to expose it to the market, that is, you have to see what someone would be willing to pay you for your bond at the time you want to sell it. To illustrate, let's say you bought $50,000 of U.S. government bonds in 1976 maturing in 20 years with regular fixed-interest payments at an annual rate of 8.5

percent. Now it is 1982, and you want to use your bonds for a down payment on a house. How much money will you get when you sell them? $50,000? $50,000 plus some percentage? more? or less? You won't know the answer until you go to the marketplace to look for a buyer.

Let's see what a buyer would be willing to offer you. Between 1976 and 1982, interest rates rose. In 1976, you could buy a bond that yielded 8.5 percent, but by 1982, you could buy a bond yielding 13 percent. When you offer to sell your $50,000 of 8.5 percent U.S. government bonds, do you think you will be able to find someone willing to pay you $50,000 for bonds that promise to pay only 8.5 percent when he or she can buy bonds paying 13 percent? The answer is no. You will find a buyer, but only at a price. The market will discount your bonds to about half of what you paid for them to even out the difference in the yield to the buyer. In 1982, you would get about $25,000 on the sale of the U.S. government bonds you bought for $50,000 in 1976.

Conversely, you can sell a bond for a profit if yields fall and your bond pays a higher yield than the market currently offers. When you sell you give up a higher income stream than is available in the current market. To buy that higher income stream, the market pays you a premium over the face amount of the bond. The bond market rally ending in the beginning of 1994 made bond investing very profitable as interest rates fell, but as interest rates rose in the balance of 1994 great sums of money were lost by bond traders.

Mutual funds investing in U.S. government bonds are volatile, since they actually buy and sell bonds for the portfolio. In addition, they are required by law to price their holdings daily, which effectively acts as a sale of the bond at current market prices for valuation purposes. The bonds with the longest maturities are most exposed to the risk of being sold at a loss in rising interest rate markets. All other things being equal, the longer the maturity of a bond portfolio, the higher the volatility. Conversely, the shorter the maturity of a bond portfolio, the lower the volatility.

WHY YOU NEED TO UNDERSTAND VOLATILITY

It is important to understand the volatility of the investment of your choice in advance of your decision to enter into a financial transaction. Volatility is your friend as you are accumulating your 401(k) wealth and your enemy when you are in your withdrawing and spending years. The downward movements of the market allow you to purchase shares of your investment at cheaper prices as you accumulate your shares. If you intend to withdraw from a volatile investment, you have to consider the possibility that you will have to sell the instrument at a much lower price than you would like. What you have to do is to manage your acquisitions and your liquidations. The rule is: Acquire into volatility and sell into stability.

As you saw in Chapter 6, the potential for wide movements in the market are present on a day to day basis. The key to managing your risk of loss when you are approaching the time you will have to retire or withdraw is to give yourself enough time so that you won't be forced to sell at a loss. This is the logic behind the rules for managing your 401(k) that I will introduce to you in the next chapter. Now, let's focus on the effect of your expected holding period on volatility and returns.

Let's consider an investment of $100 per month in an S&P Index fund. Let's look at the bands of experience assuming you invested for 10, 20, 30, and 40 years. The median reflects the center. There are as many returns above the median as there are below. Notice that the worst performance in all periods ended in a down market (1974 or 1981 in these examples).

The results of investing for a 10-year period are as follows. Keep in mind that you made 120 monthly investments of $100 each.

			ENDING VALUE	
$12,000 Invested	Low	−2%	$10,600	1965–74
	High	22%	$38,000	1946–55
	Median	12%	$22,000	1973–82

The results of investing for a 20-year period are as follows. You made 240 monthly investments of $100:

			ENDING VALUE	
$24,000 Invested	Low	4.0%	$36,500	1955–74
	High	16.5%	$160,000	1940–59
	Median	12.4%	$96,000	1969–88

Compare a 30-year period, where you made 360 investments of $100 each month:

			ENDING VALUE	
$36,000 Invested	Low	8.5%	$156,000	1952–81
	High	14.0%	$471,000	1932–61
	Median	11.5%	$274,000	1965–94

The results of investing for a 40-year period are as follows, with 48 investments of $100 per month:

			ENDING VALUE	
$48,000 Invested	Low	9.6%	$500,000	1935–74
	High	12.0%	$1,000,000	1929–68
	Median	11.0%	$755,000	1948–87

You will notice that:

1. The longer the holding period, the narrower the range of return is around the median return.
2. As the holding period lengthens, the lowest range of experience moves up from negatives to positive territory.
3. The highest returns are those that end in an up market.
4. The lowest returns for longer-term holding periods are those that end in a down market.

Does the effect of longer holding periods give you any insights you can use in managing your 401(k)?

Volatility in the stock market is very high from month to month and year to year. But time works magic in regular periodic investing. Volatility works for you and the longer holding periods smooth out the returns to the point that you have wealth beyond what you imagined you would have. Of course, this assumes you don't sell into a down market at the end of your holding period.

As a 401(k) investor, the fewer investment changes you make, the better off you will be. You should not be buying and selling your 401(k) investments on a regular basis. Normally, you would be holding them until a planned time in the future when you sell for a particular personal or portfolio reason, such as reallocating a portion of your portfolio from stocks into bonds for a conservative balance to ensure an orderly withdrawal.

VOLATILITY IN CONTEXT OF A 401(K) ACCOUNT

Let's examine how you would have done selecting a fund that invests in large company stocks for your 401(k).[2] Focusing on the highly volatile markets of 1926–38, let's follow through a single

[2] For illustration purposes. S&P Index funds did not come into existence until the 1970s.

investment of $10 to buy one $10 share of a S&P Index fund[3] in 1926. With an understanding of this period of time, you will not be affected by gloom-and-doom headlines of the type we saw on October 20, 1987, reporting the end of the U.S. capital markets.

I will consider only one of the six 401(k) compounding effects in this example, the reinvestment of dividends. I will add to that the action of market price fluctuations. The returns will include both the price of the index fund and the reinvestment of dividends.

The price of the share you purchased in a replication of a 1926–38 type market would have gone up in seven years: 1926, 1927, 1928, 1933, 1935, 1936, and 1938. It would have gone down in six years, four of which were consecutive loss years: 1929, 1930, 1931, 1932, 1934, and 1937. At no other time during 1926–95 have we experienced more than two consecutive loss years.[4]

Returns for the period in question are set out in the table below. Look at the returns and consider what you would have done if you were holding this fund in your 401(k) during these markets. Ask yourself if you would have sold the fund after seeing your $10 investment first rise to $22.04 in 1928 then fall to $7.89 in 1932. (If you looked at daily price action, you would have seen even wider swings in price.) As you look at the table below, remember it represents one $10 share purchased in 1926 and held throughout the period. The share price column shows you what you would get if you sold your share at the end of that year. This is also the *purchase price* of a share if you wanted to buy that year. The gain/loss column includes both changes in price as well as the reinvestment of dividends.

---

[3] In the market crashes of this period of time, it is borrowing activity, not price action, that caused the financial ruin of a great number of stock pickers. Margin requirements at that time were extremely low. You could put up only $5 or $10 to buy a $100 stock. If the market fell only 5 percent to 10 percent, you lost all of your investment unless you put up more margin. Today, you have to put up 50 percent of the purchase price if you want to borrow to buy stocks through your broker.

[4] In 1973 and 1974, the market went down 14.66 percent and 26.47 percent, respectively.

S&P: ONE $10 SHARE PURCHASED IN 1926 AND HELD THROUGHOUT THE PERIOD

YEAR	GAIN/LOSS (%)	GAIN/LOSS ($)	SHARE VALUE AT YEAR END
1926	11.6%	$1.16	$11.16
1927	37.5%	$4.18	$15.35
1928	43.6%	$6.69	$22.04
1929	− 8.4%	($1.86)	$20.18
1930	−24.9%	($5.03)	$15.16
1931	−43.3%	($6.57)	$8.59
1932	− 8.2%	($0.70)	$7.89
1933	54.0%	$4.26	$12.14
1934	− 1.4%	($0.17)	$11.97
1935	47.7%	$5.70	$17.67
1936	33.9%	$5.99	$23.67
1937	−35.0%	($8.29)	$15.38
1938	31.1%	$4.79	$20.16

Because you are looking at one investment held for the long term, your year-to-year changes will fluctuate with the market, but your investment return will be determined by the difference between your purchase price ($10) and your selling price at the time you choose to sell. For example, the greatest loss year (1931) was down 43 percent from the previous year (1930). If you had sold in 1931 the cumulative loss on your investment of $10 would have been 14 percent ($10 − $8.59 = $1.41), not 43 percent.

If you had sold at the end of 1938, the gain on your original $10 investment would have been $10.16, for a 101 percent cumulative profit ($20.16 − $10 = $10.16 or 101 percent). Your average annual return would have been 7.8 percent. If you had sold in 1968, after holding for 43 years, your selling price would have been $656.41, for an average annual return of 12.6 percent. If you had sold at the end of 1978, your average annual return would have been 11.2 percent. If you had sold in 1988, your average annual return would have been 12 percent.

Most investors lose their resolve to continue to hold a more volatile investment such as the S&P fund in a down year such as 1932, when they compare what they would have had in a less volatile investment such as Treasuries. What would you have done if after seven years your $10 index fund investment was worth $7.89, while your Treasury bill was worth $12?

Better yet, what would you have done if after seven years, your $10 small stock mutual fund investment was worth only $2.45 in comparison to your $12 Treasury bill?

In order to get a better frame of reference, let's look at longer market periods and let's compare both Treasury bills and small stocks to the S&P.

For a direct comparison to the previous S&P example, we will show Treasury bill interest income under the Gain/Loss column in the table and the reinvestment of interest as part of the "Share Price." You will see in the following table that there are no down years in terms of share price. But you will also see that the benefit of having stability of principal has a price: lack of growth.

TREASURY BILLS: ONE $10 "SHARE" PURCHASED IN 1926 AND HELD THROUGHOUT THE PERIOD

YEAR	GAIN/LOSS (%)	GAIN/LOSS ($)	SHARE PRICE
1926	3.3%	$0.33	$10.33
1927	3.1%	$0.32	$10.65
1928	3.6%	$0.38	$11.03
1929	4.7%	$0.52	$11.55
1930	2.4%	$0.28	$11.83
1931	1.1%	$0.13	$11.96
1932	0.9%	$0.11	$12.07
1933	0.3%	$0.04	$12.11
1934	0.2%	$0.02	$12.13
1935	0.1%	$0.02	$12.15
1936	0.2%	$0.02	$12.17
1937	0.3%	$0.04	$12.21
1938	0.0%	$0.00	$12.21

If you had sold your Treasury bill "share" at the end of 1938, the gain on your original $10 investment would have been $2.21. Your average annual return would have been 1.6 percent. If you had sold in 1968, after holding for 43 years, your selling price would have been $21.00 for an average annual return of 1.7 percent. If you had sold at the end of 1978, your average annual return would have been 2.5 percent. If you had sold in 1988, your average annual return would have been 3.5 percent.

Question: How do Treasury bill returns for the period 1926–95 compare to S&P returns?

Answer: Average annual returns for the S&P were approximately 12 percent, compared to 3.7 percent for Treasury bills. But this higher return for the S&P came with a cost: interim fluctuations in price.

Let's compare one more asset class, small stocks, as we have defined them. You might come across small stocks as one of your 401(k) selections as a small stock fund or a growth stock fund.

SMALL STOCKS: ONE $10 SHARE PURCHASED IN 1926 AND HELD THROUGHOUT THE PERIOD

YEAR	GAIN/LOSS (%)	GAIN/LOSS ($)	SHARE PRICE
1926	0.3%	$0.03	$10.03
1927	22.1%	$2.22	$12.24
1928	39.7%	$4.86	$17.10
1929	−51.4%	($8.78)	$8.32
1930	−38.2%	($3.17)	$5.15
1931	−49.8%	($2.56)	$2.59
1932	−5.4%	($0.14)	$2.45
1933	142.9%	$3.49	$5.94
1934	24.2%	$1.44	$7.38
1935	40.2%	$2.97	$10.35
1936	64.8%	$6.70	$17.05
1937	−58.0%	($9.89)	$7.16
1938	32.8%	$2.35	$9.51

If you had sold at the end of 1938, the loss on your original $10 investment would have been $0.49. Your average annual return would have been 12 percent, which shows you can have a positive average annual return and no gain. If you had sold in 1968, after holding for 43 years, your selling price would have been over $1,600 for an average annual return of 19.33 percent. If you had sold at the end of 1978, your selling price would have been over $2,600 and your average annual return would have been 17 percent. If you had sold in 1988, your average annual return would have been 17.79 percent and your selling price would have been over $14,000.

Question: How does this market compare to the S&P and Treasuries?

Answer: Small stocks are much more volatile than the S&P, reflecting average annual returns of 18 percent and a standard deviation of 35 percent, compared to a standard deviation of 20 percent for the S&P. Standard deviation is a statistical term that shows variation around a mean. The higher the standard deviation, the higher the volatility.

What can you conclude from this comparison of price volatility of different asset classes?

1. In volatile markets, stock prices move dramatically, up and down.
2. If you wanted to cut your losses in a bad market by selling, you might think twice and buy instead.
3. If you invest in volatile market instruments, you had better be prepared to ride out bad markets.
4. In very bad markets, it can take a long time to recover your original investment.
5. If you are investing for the long term, interim price movements have less significance, even in widely fluctuating markets.
6. If you want your assets to grow, you have to assume market risk.
7. Nonvolatile investments such as Treasury bills have the advantage over stocks if you want stability of principal.
8. Volatile investments such as stocks have an advantage over Treasury bills if you want to grow your assets.
9. Small stocks have proven to be more volatile than stocks of large companies and have shown higher long-term returns.

COMPARING INVESTMENT VOLATILITY OF A 401(K) TO A REGULAR ACCOUNT

In previous chapters, I compared a regular investment account to a 401(k) for purposes of illustrating the six compounding factors. Now let's look at whether there is any difference between a regular account, a 401(k) with no match, and a 401(k) with a 100 percent match when it comes to risk as defined by volatility. As you might guess, volatility dampens, or lessens, the more compounding elements you have available to you.

Consider how Holly's regular account would have done in an S&P Index fund, starting with an investment made in 1926 and assuming an annual investment of $1,560, plus the 3 percent she added each year because of salary increases. Lacking the Pretax Advantage, only $1,170 of her $1,560 is available for investing, since Holly must first pay taxes on her earnings. Holly's highest and lowest account values for the period are highlighted in the table below. You will notice that in each year of market decline, Holly's account value drops below the amount she invested. In the worst year, 1931, Holly's cumulative investment was $7,568, but her account value fell to $4,110. In the best year, 1936, Holly had invested $14,985, and her account value had grown to $22,375. In a regular account only one compounding element is available, the Reinvestment Privilege.

REGULAR ACCOUNT, S&P

YEAR	GAIN/LOSS (%)	ENDING VALUE	HOLLY'S CUMULATIVE CONTRIBUTIONS
1926	11.6%	$1,272	$1,170
1927	37.5%	$3,174	$2,375
1928	43.6%	$5,859	$3,616
1929	−8.4%	$6,536	$4,895
1930	−24.9%	$5,898	$6,212
1931	−43.3%	$4,110	$7,568
1932	−8.2%	$5,056	$8,965
1933	54.0%	$9,125	$10,404
1934	−1.4%	$10,455	$11,886
1935	47.7%	$16,265	$13,413
1936	33.9%	$22,375	$14,985
1937	−35.0%	$15,589	$16,605
1938	31.1%	$21,285	$18,273

Now let's look at the effect of adding the benefits of the Pretax Advantage and Tax-Deferred Growth that the 401(k) offers. To simplify the illustrations, we are not showing the Leveraged Paycheck. For this example, her 401(k) does not have a match.

You will notice that market decline years had less impact on ending values than they did for the regular account, due to the effect of the added compounding factors.

401(K), NO MATCH, S&P

YEAR	GAIN/LOSS (%)	ENDING VALUE	HOLLY'S CUMULATIVE CONTRIBUTIONS
1926	11.6%	$1,741	$1,560
1927	37.5%	$4,603	$3,167
1928	43.6%	$8,987	$4,822
1929	−8.4%	$9,792	$6,526
1930	−24.9%	$8,672	$8,282
1931	−43.3%	$5,938	$10,091
1932	−8.2%	$7,162	$11,953
1933	54.0%	$13,984	$13,872
1934	−1.4%	$15,730	$15,848
1935	47.7%	$26,234	$17,884
1936	33.9%	$37,940	$19,980
1937	−35.0%	$26,053	$22,140
1938	31.1%	$37,077	$24,364

If Holly had sold her holdings in the largest loss year, 1931, she would have lost $4,153 or 41 percent of her cumulative investment ($10,091 − $5,938 = $4,153). If Holly had sold her investment in 1936, for $37,940, her gain would have been $17,960 or 47 percent ($37,940 − $19,980 = $17,960).

Finally, let's add two more compounding elements to the equation by assuming that Holly's plan has a match. As in previous illustrations of Holly's 401(k), in Chapter 2, we will assume a match of 100 percent. In the following table, you can see that the wide market fluctuations had much less impact on her results because of the effect of the added compounding elements. Even in 1931, the greatest decline year, the ending value is higher than Holly's cumulative contributions. (For purposes of demonstrating volatility in a 401(k), I am assuming immediate vesting of the company match. In your case, if your match does not vest for five years, you cannot count on it until you actually vest, since you lose the match if you leave the employ of your company before then.)

401(K), 100% MATCH, S&P

YEAR	GAIN/LOSS (%)	ENDING VALUE	HOLLY'S CUMULATIVE CONTRIBUTIONS
1926	11.6%	$3,483	$1,560
1927	37.5%	$9,207	$3,167
1928	43.6%	$17,975	$4,822
1929	−8.4%	$19,584	$6,526
1930	−24.9%	$17,345	$8,282
1931	−43.3%	$11,877	$10,091
1932	−8.2%	$14,324	$11,953
1933	54.0%	$27,967	$13,872
1934	−1.4%	$31,460	$15,848
1935	47.7%	$52,468	$17,884
1936	33.9%	$75,881	$19,980
1937	−35.0%	$52,106	$22,140
1938	31.1%	$74,154	$24,364

MEASURING RETURNS

Measuring the ups and downs of your account will give you the volatility of your account, but not your returns. To measure your returns, you have to compare how much you invested to how much you received when you sold. With a 401(k) you should not need to sell your holdings until you make asset class reallocations in preparation for withdrawals.

There are important lessons to be learned from these tables.

First, volatility lessens or dampens with time.

Second, volatility also dampens with the addition of compounding elements.

Third, when dealing with a broad market investment such as an index fund, you can manage your returns by managing *when you sell*.

Fourth, investors measure their real returns based on a comparison of what they invested and what they received when they liquidated.

WITHDRAWALS

From the above discussion of volatility you can see that when you sell your holdings will determine your returns. In a 401(k), you will not be trading your account for short-term gains. Instead, you will be building an asset base during the time you are working, so that you can convert those holdings to an income stream for retirement. I will provide you with the methodology for accomplishing that result in the next chapter. For now, you need to be aware that the timing of your liquidation of 401(k) holdings will be critical to your results.

MORE RECENT MARKET PERIODS

When you start your investment analysis with the worst market periods, you develop a perspective on how you can use those markets to fulfill your goals. Understanding risk is essential to successful investing.

The decades that followed the Depression had fewer loss years and year-over-year price fluctuations were less wide. In the forties, there were three loss years, with the largest loss being 11.6 percent and the largest gain being 36 percent. In the fifties, there were two loss years, with the largest loss being 11 percent and the largest gain being 53 percent. In the sixties, there were three loss years, the largest loss being 10 percent and the largest gain 27 percent. In the seventies, there were three loss years, with the largest loss being 26 percent and the largest gain 37 percent. In the eighties, there was only one loss year, with a 5 percent loss (1981) and three years of over 30 percent gains. In the nineties, to date, there has been one loss year (1990) and five up years, two of which were over 30 percent.

The arithmetic average for the entire period (1926–95) is 12 percent per year. Notably, this period is inclusive of the 1929 crash and the Depression years, as well as the crash of 1987. The figure represents changes in prices in stocks as well as dividends paid by the companies and reinvested into additional shares of stock.

COMPARING MORE VOLATILE INSTRUMENTS

The changes in S&P returns year to year illustrate the concept of volatility. Up and down movement in price — volatility — is a measure of risk. As you can conclude from the above discussion, it is important to understand volatility when you are considering investment options.

It will be important for you to compare the volatility of the various investment options you can select from. Let's compare the volatility of the small-stock market to the S&P 500 Index.

The most volatile period for the S&P was the Depression. The same was true for the small-stock market.

Do you remember the largest year-to-year loss for the S&P? (Answer: Down 43 percent in 1931.)

The small-stock market had its greatest loss of 58 percent, in 1937. There were two more loss years of similar magnitude in 1929 and 1931, and a 38 percent loss in 1930.

The following table shows the 20 largest year-to-year losses arranged from highest to lowest and the years in which they occurred. In addition, in this market, during this 70-year period (1926–95) there were 21 loss years in comparison to 20 loss years in the S&P.

You can see that losses in the small-stock market were much more significant than losses in the large company stock market as measured by the S&P. As you would expect, the gains were larger, as well, which illustrates again the importance of understanding comparative volatility of asset classes.

LARGEST 20 YEAR-TO-YEAR LOSSES IN THE STOCK MARKET

	S&P		SMALL STOCKS	
1.	1931	−43.3%	1937	−58.0%
2.	1937	−35.0%	1929	−51.4%
3.	1974	−26.5%	1931	−49.8%
4.	1930	−24.9%	1930	−38.2%
5.	1973	−14.7%	1973	−30.9%
6.	1941	−11.6%	1969	−25.1%
7.	1957	−10.8%	1990	−21.6%
8.	1966	−10.1%	1974	−20.0%
9.	1940	−9.8%	1970	−17.4%
10.	1962	−8.7%	1957	−14.6%
11.	1969	−8.5%	1962	−11.9%
12.	1929	−8.4%	1946	−11.6%
13.	1932	−8.2%	1987	−9.3%
14.	1946	−8.1%	1941	−9.0%
15.	1977	−7.2%	1966	−7.0%
16.	1981	−4.9%	1984	−6.7%
17.	1990	−3.2%	1953	−6.5%
18.	1934	−1.4%	1932	−5.4%
19.	1953	−1.0%	1940	−5.2%
20.	1939	−0.4%	1960	−3.3%

You can compare the higher gains afforded by the small-stock market in the following table, which is arranged in order of the 20 highest gains in both asset classes. You'll notice that a number of the highest and lowest years occurred in the 1920s and 1930s, and you'll see the upward bias of the market.

LARGEST 20 YEAR-TO-YEAR GAINS IN THE STOCK MARKET

	S&P		SMALL STOCKS	
1.	1933	54.0%	1933	142.9%
2.	1954	52.6%	1943	88.4%
3.	1935	47.7%	1967	83.6%
4.	1928	43.6%	1945	73.6%
5.	1958	43.4%	1958	64.9%
6.	1927	37.5%	1936	64.8%
7.	1995	37.4%	1954	60.6%
8.	1975	37.2%	1976	57.4%
9.	1945	36.4%	1944	53.7%
10.	1936	33.9%	1975	52.8%
11.	1980	32.4%	1991	44.6%
12.	1985	32.2%	1942	44.5%
13.	1950	31.7%	1979	43.5%
14.	1955	31.6%	1965	41.8%
15.	1989	31.5%	1935	40.2%
16.	1938	31.1%	1980	39.9%
17.	1991	30.6%	1928	39.7%
18.	1961	26.9%	1983	39.7%
19.	1943	25.9%	1950	38.8%
20.	1951	24.0%	1968	36.0%

If you look at the lowest-performing years in these markets, you can get a good sense of what you might expect in the worst of times. If you look at the best years, you can get a sense of what you might expect in the best of times. Stock investing involves buying and selling stocks in order to build capital. No one, professional investors included, can pick one winning stock after another. The reason for this is that there is no consistently successful way to predict the price movement of a particular stock or the stock market as a whole. If you could predict whether a stock would go up over the next period of time, investing would be a lot simpler. But you can't do that, because stock prices move based on a myriad of factors, many of which are not quantifiable. Hence you have to live with some uncertainty when it comes to the price movement of a stock or the market generally.

In investing, risk is not to be avoided, but understood and managed. No one can predict the direction of the stock market consistently for any length of time. It would be a mistake for you place your 401(k) money on that kind of a bet.

What you do know with certainty is that prices of stocks will fluctuate. You know that no one can tell you reliably and consistently whether the market will go up or down on any particular day. You know that your 401(k) investments need to be able to give you a positive real rate of return over inflation. You know that those types of investments come with a price, volatility. You know that you will need money to live on in retirement. You know that it is unlikely that pension and Social Security income will be sufficient in most cases to cover the gap between expenses and income in retirement. You know that your 401(k) is one of the best ways to get you the results you need.

Don't try to shift your holdings in anticipation of a market move. Develop a game plan for all markets and stick to it. Be disciplined and have confidence in your plan. In the next chapter, I will set out a methodology for you to use to make your investment selections work for you.

8

The 401(k) Phase
Portfolio Strategy

Understanding risk is an important step toward managing your 401(k). The next tool you need is an overall portfolio strategy. The secret to managing your investment portfolio is understanding that there are three phases in the 401(k), and that each is governed by a different set of investment objectives. To be successful, you need to choose investments that properly line up with the investment objectives applicable to your stage in the 401(k) cycle.

The three 401(k) phases are accumulation, rebalancing, and withdrawal. First, I will define these stages and the primary investment objective that governs. Each stage may also have one or more secondary objectives that depend on the investment selections available to you, whether your match is made in cash or company stock, and other factors outside your 401(k). I will discuss primary objectives first and secondary objectives later in this chapter as well as the methodology you need to use to match your investment selections to your objectives.

THE ACCUMULATION STAGE

When you enroll in your 401(k) and begin to participate, you are in the beginning stages of the accumulation phase of your plan. During this stage, your purpose is to accumulate 401(k) assets.

The accumulation phase is the period of time during which you are either funding your plan with contributions or allowing the plan to develop due to the reinvestment of dividends, capital gains, or interest.

The length of the accumulation phase varies from person to person. If you are 25, your accumulation phase may last 40 years until you are 65 (or 46 years until you are 70½). If you are 55, your accumulation phase will last 10 to 15 years.

In the accumulation phase of your plan, your primary investment objective is to grow capital. Your secondary objective will depend on your particular situation. For example, if your plan pays a match in company stock, you may need diversification as your secondary objective. Another example of a secondary objective is to add one or more investment vehicles that can lessen or lower the volatility of your accumulation portfolio.

THE REBALANCING STAGE

The rebalancing phase of your 401(k) life cycle is the time period between accumulation and withdrawal. The length of this phase depends on a number of factors at play in the particular investment account. Normally, the rebalancing phase should last three to four years before withdrawals begin. The rebalancing phase prepares your portfolio for the production of income.

The primary investment objective during your rebalancing phase is to move from a capital-producing portfolio to an income-producing portfolio. The speed at which you rebalance will depend on your circumstances. For example, if you are holding a high concentration of company stock because of a company match, you will need to be especially careful in assessing the time during which you should rebalance based on the market characteristics of your stock.

THE WITHDRAWAL STAGE

Every action you take in your plan leads up to this stage, the withdrawal phase. The withdrawal phase usually lasts 20, 30 years or longer. Optimally, withdrawals would begin at age 70½, when minimum withdrawals are mandated by the tax laws. However, withdrawals can begin as early as 59½ without early withdrawal penalties. When you are in the withdrawal phase, you want to be able to pay yourself a "pension" check out of your 401(k).

In retirement your primary investment objective is to produce income. Your secondary objective will depend on your particular circumstances. For example, if your 401(k) is not large enough to support you throughout retirement, you may have a secondary objective to commit 20 percent of your 401(k) portfolio to growth of capital.

You have every opportunity to do well with your 401(k) investments as long as you keep your 401(k) objectives in sight. To be successful, you have to do only one thing: Make certain that each buy, hold, and sell decision lines up properly with your current target. As a 401(k) investor, your overall strategic objective is to accumulate an asset base large enough to support you in retirement. Depending on where you are in your 401(k) cycle, your current objective may be to grow capital, produce income, or rebalance in preparation for producing income.

CHARACTERISTICS OF INVESTMENT SELECTIONS

Each of the investment selections offered by your plan has a different set of investment characteristics. The characteristics define whether there is a fit, that is, whether their investment characteristics move you toward your investment objective.

Investment selections that are appropriate for the production of income are typically less suited for the growth of capital. For example, a guaranteed investment contract paying a fixed rate of return may be more suited for the production of income in your withdrawal phase and less suited for the growth of capital in the accumulation phase. Thus, in a normal interest rate market you might not choose a guaranteed investment contract as your core holding for your accumulation phase. (In high interest rate markets, more seasoned 401(k) investors might use earnings from income-producing instruments to purchase growth instruments, thus effectively changing the character of the strategy to growth as opposed to income. For most individuals who are investing through their 401(k)s, it would be a mistake to mix objectives in this manner.)

However, the guaranteed investment contract might fulfill a secondary objective of your accumulation phase, for example, to lessen volatility or to diversify your holdings. In addition, the guaranteed investment contract might be a good choice for you when you are in the withdrawal phase or the rebalancing phase, this time as a core holding.

Likewise, an investment selection that is appropriate for growth of capital may not be best suited for the production of income. For example, by definition, a growth fund does not produce income and will not be suited as your primary holding in your withdrawal phase when your primary investment objective is to produce income. On the other hand, the growth fund may be appropriate for you when you are in your accumulation phase when your primary investment objective is to grow capital. A growth fund might meet a secondary objective of growing capital, in any phase, even in the withdrawal phase.

Generally, you will be able to assess the investment objective of your particular selection and match it to the primary and secondary investment objectives of your particular phase. Depending on the number and characteristics of your investment selections, you will be able to choose one or more investments to accomplish each of your primary and secondary investment objectives.

To give you an example of how these considerations might come together, if you are 25 years old, you should be looking at 35 to 40 years of accumulation. Let's say you have a generous match of 100 percent that is paid in cash (not company stock), and you have done your research regarding your investment selections. In addition, you understand the volatility of your investment choices and are willing to live through down markets.

In a case such as this, there would be no portfolio reason to have any holdings in money markets or fixed-income holdings at age 25. All your holdings could justifiably be in the stock market. The percentage allocations would depend on the character of your investment options, which is the subject of our discussion in the next chapter. As you invest each month, you would continue to add to these holdings until you are 55 or so. Again, much of what you will do will depend on the investment offerings available to you. In addition, you would start adding a third asset class to your holdings, a hybrid fund in the income or balanced fund category. When you are 60, you would add appropriate bond funds at the time, such as shorter-term, high-quality bond funds.

If you do not intend to use your 401(k) assets until mandatory distribution begins at age 70½, you will hold on to all of your positions, all the time reinvesting dividends, until you are 67 or so. At that time, you will reassess your holdings and the market and begin to rebalance your portfolio in anticipation of minimum withdrawals beginning at age 70½. In any case, you will want to manage your withdrawals so that all or most come from the dividends generated by your fixed-income holdings, which now should constitute a larger part of your portfolio. The exact percentage will depend on your financial needs, the size of the 401(k), and your other tax-deferred holdings. If there is insufficient dividend income for your mandatory distributions, they should come from liquidations of less volatile holdings, such as short-term bond funds in your portfolio or even money market funds.

In the above scenario, in a plan with a generous match, between the ages of 25 and 55, I might suggest directing 60 percent of your contributions into the broad market and 40 percent into the growth stock market. From 55 through 60, you would direct 100 percent into income funds or balanced funds. From 60 until retirement, you would direct 100 percent into fixed-income funds. At 67, you would begin exchanging some (not all) of your stock holdings into fixed-income holdings, the amounts and times varying according to your assessment of the markets, your other tax-deferred holdings, and your income needs at age 70 and beyond.

- Ages 25–55: *Invest 60 percent of your current contributions in growth and income funds and 40 percent in growth stock funds.*
- Ages 55–60: *Invest 100 percent of your current contribution in income funds or balanced funds.*
- Ages 60–65: *Invest 100 percent of your current contributions in bond funds.*
- Ages 65–67: *Hold all positions, reinvesting dividends.*
- Ages 67–70: *Begin a planned program of exchanging some (not all) stock funds to bond funds.*
- Age 71 and beyond: *Withdraw from dividends only, as long as if possible.*

If you are just starting to participate in your 401(k) at age 50 or over, you may need to extend your accumulation phase to age 60 or 65, depending on when you plan to start to withdraw from your 401(k). Remember that you need to cushion potential losses by rebalancing before you begin your withdrawals, so allow yourself plenty of time to move into income-producing holdings before taking money out of your 401(k).

In Chapter 9, I will look more closely at the various holdings that might be available to you and help you assess the investment selections in your plan. I will also show you how to make appropriate matches depending on where you are in your 401(k) investment cycle and how to monitor your investments and make adjustments when necessary.

9

How to Choose Investments
That Are Right for You

Your company's management has reviewed, analyzed, and chosen a selection of investment offerings for your plan. Selections may include a number of mutual funds, investment pools managed by an investment adviser or bank, annuities, your company's stock, and possibly guaranteed investment contracts, which are contractual obligations of insurance companies. Your task is comparing the options before you and choosing those that best suit your needs based on your 401(k) phase. In this chapter, I will show you the selection criteria to use and the methodology to follow in making your selections.

FIRST SELECTION CRITERION: PURPOSE

The most important assessment for you to make is the purpose of each of your available options. You can assess the purpose of a particular investment through an understanding of "investment objectives." The investment objectives of a fund tell the investment manager the goal he or she needs to attain in the job of investing the assets of the fund.

If you understand the investment objectives, you will understand the proper use to which the investment can be put in your 401(k). Remember that the key is to match the investment's

116

objectives to *your* objectives as you and your 401(k) move through the 401(k) life cycle.

All 401(k) investment selections offered to you by your plan serve one of three *primary* purposes: (1) to grow your capital, (2) to produce an income stream for you in retirement, or (3) to do both. You can categorize every investment option available to you based on its effectiveness in accomplishing these results. Some of your selections can also serve one of three *secondary* purposes in your 401(k) portfolio: (1) reducing the volatility of your overall portfolio, (2) diversifying your overall portfolio if you have a match or profit-sharing contribution paid in company stock, and (3) providing a temporary parking place in anticipation of a withdrawal. Typically, money market funds are used for this purpose.

Keep in mind that most of your working career, you are in the accumulation phase of your 401(k) life cycle, and your *primary* objective is to grow your assets. During the accumulation phase, you do not need your portfolio to produce income, and in fact, you are prohibited by tax penalties from taking income out of your 401(k) during this time. Depending on your situation, you may have a *secondary* objective to diversify your portfolio or to lower the volatility of your overall holdings with income-producing holdings.

You will need your portfolio to produce income when you retire. At that time you will be in the withdrawal phase of your 401(k). Your *primary* investment objective will be to produce income. Depending on the size of your portfolio and your needs, you may also have a *secondary* objective to grow capital.

Before you retire, you will enter the rebalancing phase of your 401(k) life cycle, which is sandwiched between the accumulation phase and the withdrawal phase. During your rebalancing phase, you will need to reposition your portfolio from one that produces growth of capital to one that produces income for you to live on in retirement.

Examples

You will find that investments that have the objective of growing capital are composed of stocks (equities) and those that have the objectives of producing income are comprised primarily of bonds (fixed-income instruments). There is a third category, which I would call a hybrid. The hybrid category invests in *both* stocks and bonds and is intended to produces *both* capital and income. The hybrid category is typically less volatile than the growth of capital category.

Generally, mutual funds and investment pools that invest in stocks fall into the growth of capital category, as would your company stock. Funds that invest in bonds fall into the income category. Funds that invest in both stocks and bonds fall into the hybrid category, having the objective of both growth of capital and the production of income.

1. Examples of the *growth of capital* category are a stock index fund, a growth stock fund, a growth and income fund, a small cap fund, a value fund, or any other type of stock mutual fund that has as its stated investment objective the growth of capital. (Note that the "growth and income" fund is not normally a hybrid fund. The name, growth and income, denotes that the fund invests in large company stocks that pay dividends.)

2. Examples of the *income* category are a short-term, intermediate-term, or long-term bond fund, a government bond fund, a GNMA fund (Ginnie-Mae), or any other type of fixed-income mutual fund that has income as its stated investment objective. I would also include in this category money market funds as well as guaranteed investment contracts. The commonality is the focus on the production of income as opposed to growth of capital. An additional characteristic of money market funds and guaranteed investment contracts is their objective of seeking to maintain stability of principal. These two investment vehicles will

probably be the only two selections available to you with a stable asset value regardless of market conditions.

3. Examples of the *hybrid category* are an income fund or a balanced fund. Lifestyle funds and asset allocation funds are not technically hybrid funds, although there is no better way to categorize them.

Looking at your investment selections in this way, you will see that some investment options might be better suited than others to accomplishing the particular objectives you are seeking at your phase of your 401(k). For example, you might find that a money market fund will be the least useful to you in building capital. However, depending on your remaining choices and the current market, your money market fund might be most suitable for a secondary objective, such as lowering the volatility of your 401(k) portfolio.

Your Investment Options

Let's look at your 401(k) investment options. Start with the list of investment options available to you under your plan. Find a description of each of the options. The best source for objectives is the prospectus, which you can get from your administrator. If you haven't read your prospectuses, this is a good time to take a look at them. The process is simple if you know how to approach it.

First, you want to quickly assess the purpose of the fund — its investment objective. Investment objectives are described in the front of the prospectus. In some prospectuses, the investment objective is highlighted on the cover of the prospectus.

For example, the cover of the Growth Fund of America prospectus states the fund offers "an opportunity for growth of capital through a diversified portfolio of common stocks." Franklin's AGE High Income Fund seeks high current income. The Vanguard Explorer Fund seeks "long-term growth in capital." The Vanguard Admiral U.S. Treasury Money Market Portfolio seeks "to provide current income consistent with the preservation of capital and liquidity." The inside cover of the Vanguard Asset Allocation Fund states the fund "seeks to maximize total return (i.e. capital change plus income)." The Investment Company of America cover states the fund offers "an opportunity for long-term growth of capital and income." (Please note that these are examples and not recommendations.)

You can see from this very quick look that initial categorization by use will not be difficult. In fact, you will find that you can put all your options into three broad categories based on their stated purposes: (1) those that are meant to grow your capital, (2) those that are meant to provide income, and (3) those that seek to do both.

In looking at the funds mentioned above, you would put easily categorize them as follows:

1. **Grow capital:** Growth Fund of America and Vanguard Explorer Fund
2. **Produce income:** Franklin's AGE High Income Fund and Vanguard Admiral U.S. Treasury Money Market (This last fund can also be categorized as "preserving your capital.")
3. **Grow capital *and* produce income:** Vanguard Asset Allocation Fund and Investment Company of America

Based solely on a top-level assessment of investment objectives, you can see that funds are organized for different purposes. As a general rule, in your accumulation phase you would want to choose investments intended to grow capital, which would include choices in categories one and three. As a general rule, in your withdrawal phase, you would want to choose investments intended to produce income, which would include choices in categories two and three. In the rebalancing phase, you would generally want to start replacing investments in category one with investments in categories two and three. This assessment is the first level of your inquiry, allowing you to get a sense of how you might use your investment options for your purposes. We will explain additional selection criteria that you need to apply shortly.

You can use the following table to categorize the investment options available to you. In the Category Column, put (1) growth, (2) income, or (3) growth and income.

INVESTMENT OPTION	INVESTMENT OBJECTIVE	CATEGORY

Understanding the objectives of your fund offerings helps you categorize them so that you can assess how you might use them. This is the first level of your inquiry. The second level of inquiry is volatility.

SECOND SELECTION CRITERION: VOLATILITY

In Chapters 6 and 7 I discussed the different elements of risk. At this point, you need to be able to array your selections from lowest to highest volatility. Generally your least volatile investment selections will be your income-producing investments.

This is the order of volatility by investment objective from least volatile to most volatile:

1. Money market fund
2. Guaranteed investment contract
3. Short-term bond funds
4. Intermediate-term bond funds
5. Income or balanced funds (or long-term bond funds) (note that the order of 5 and 6 depends on the length of maturity and credit of the portfolio)
6. Long-term bond funds (or income or balanced funds)
7. Growth and income funds
8. Growth funds
9. Aggressive growth funds
10. Company stock

Funds investing overseas are not included in the chart because they have additional risks due to currency exchange fluctuations. While these funds may be appropriate for diversification purposes, you would not want to have your 401(k) concentrated in overseas investments.

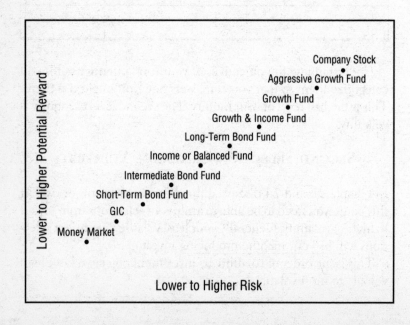

By arraying your options in this manner, you will be able to get a quick assessment of the overall volatility you might expect from your investment options. This assessment will allow you to determine the overall volatility of your portfolio, including your company match account. There are instances in which you may want to lower the overall volatility of your portfolio as a secondary objective. By arraying your investment selection in this manner, you will be able to assess which investment selections to use to move down the risk/reward grid.

You can array your holdings in the following chart.

If you are in the accumulation phase of your 401(k) life cycle and you are under the age of 35, there should be no reason to move down the risk/reward grid. When you are 55, on the other hand, you might want to do so, particularly if your match is made in company stock.

Putting It All Together

After you review your investment options, assess their purpose, and array them based on risk, you will have a good feel for how you might use each of your options.

Depending on where you are in your 401(k) cycle, you will have a possible selection of one, two, or three options that meet your primary objective. If you are 30 years old in the accumulation phase of your 401(k), you might find most suitable a growth fund, a growth and income fund, and an aggressive growth fund. Now you will have to determine which of these options you will choose to fulfill your primary objective of growth. Based on your risk array, you should be able to determine which of these three choices are most volatile. It would be quite appropriate to choose one or more of these options, and to diversify by adding a fixed-income option.

With that strategy in mind, you might direct 50 percent of your contributions into growth and income, 40 percent into growth, and 10 percent into fixed-income. If you wished to diversify more, you might increase the bond contribution to a higher percentage and lower the stock percentages. If you did not care to diversify into bonds, you might direct 50 percent into growth and income and 50 percent into growth.

The percentage allocation into your chosen asset classes will be a judgment call that you will have to make based on your understanding of your objectives, risk, and the options available to you. There is no right or wrong here in terms of percentage allocations as long as you base your choices on where you are in your 401(k) cycle and match your objectives to the objectives of the vehicles available to you.

The investment choices within an asset class will differ based on how the portfolios are managed. As you become more and more experienced in your selection process, you will become more adept at distinguishing between the investment options within an asset class. For example, one growth fund will differ from another growth fund based on how the manager's responsibilities are defined. What he or she can and cannot do with the portfolio is set out by the investment policies and limitations of the investment option you are considering. Reading prospectuses and financial reports and following performance in different types of markets will help you become more and more familiar with the instruments. Over time, your confidence will develop as you read, observe, and monitor your portfolio.

In terms of your 401(k) cycle, the toughest choices for you will be your rebalancing and withdrawal phases. When you are 50 or so, you might want to start looking at your fixed-income and hybrid choices. Also remember that you will be able to roll over your 401(k) into an IRA of your choosing when you retire, should you wish to have a broader array of investment choices available to you. If you do roll over, you will need to develop well-reasoned screening criteria for your IRA investments. For example, you will want to find bonds or bond funds that offer sufficient income with acceptable credit risk and volatility. In addition, you will probably want to continue holding some equity positions for growth throughout your retirement. You will need to assess your account in the context of all your other holdings and your anticipated cash flows during retirement, after factoring in loss of purchasing power due to inflation. Depending on your investment experience and skill, this is a time when it may be to your advantage to retain an investment adviser to guide you in asset allocation, selection of appropriate investments and to monitor progress.

Start to think in terms of how you would rebalance your holdings. When you rebalance, you are actually selling some of your accumulation vehicles and buying income vehicles. It will be important for you to make good decisions about when you sell. What you want to do is assess the markets and sell when prices are higher rather than lower. You will never be able to pick the most opportune time to sell. But with most diversified stock investments, you will be able to avoid selling into a bad market, by waiting. That is why it is important to start to think in terms of rebalancing well in advance of your need to sell at withdrawal time.

As long as you remember to accumulate into volatility and withdraw from stability, you will be able to protect your asset base when you need to. For example, let's say your primary holding is a stock index fund and you are 55 years old. The market drops approximately 20 percent in one year and another 20 percent the next year, reminiscent of 1973–74. You would not rebalance your portfolio at that time. You would wait and begin rebalancing in more favorable markets.

Let's say you are 70½ and you need to begin withdrawals. Now, you are forced into a liquidation at disadvantageous prices. You want to be able to avoid this result by rebalancing well before you need to withdraw.

When you are ready to withdraw, your portfolio should be heavily weighted in income-producing instruments, with some element of growth. The amount of growth will depend on your income needs and your other non-401(k) holdings. Ideally, you want to withdraw through dividend or interest payments instead of principal liquidations. If this is your strategy, you would be able to figure out your asset allocations working back from your dividend expectations.

As you can see from this discussion, putting together a 401(k) portfolio is a matter of understanding where you are and where you are going. It is a dynamic exercise. Your portfolio evolves as your needs evolve. At this point, you might want to revisit Chapter 8 to review the 401(k) phases and develop rules you will follow from today until you start to withdraw from your 401(k).

10

Managing Withdrawals for Maximum Income in Retirement

One of the 10 advantages of a 401(k) is the ability to continue tax-deferred growth after you retire and begin to withdraw from your account. Managing the effect of income taxes on withdrawals is an important aspect of maximizing your 401(k) benefits.

Retirement is the time to put your 401(k) retirement assets to work for you to produce retirement income. You can take a lump-sum distribution from your account and pay your taxes in full all at once. Or you can take advantage of tax laws that let keep your taxes low and your income high.

Before retirement, you will need to review your taxes with your tax adviser in detail to choose the best alternative for your particular situation. The following discussion will show you one of the methods available to you and how it might be an improvement over a lump-sum distribution.

In Chapter 2, you saw Holly take a lump-sum distribution at age 65 and pay taxes on the distribution in full. We saw Holly's $1,560 contribution a year grow to $1.5 million, without any increases in her contributions due to increases in salary. Her lump-sum distribution was $1.5 million. We showed income taxes at a low 25 percent rate ($375,000) and compared a higher 45 percent tax rate ($675,000).

Let's look more closely at her option to continue tax-deferred growth into retirement. In order to do that, Holly needs to either stay in her plan or roll over her 401(k) account into an IRA. She decides she wants to hold off on taking money out of her account until age 70½, which is the longest she can wait by law.

From age 65 through age 70, Holly rebalances her portfolio into less volatile investments. By age 71, assuming a 6 percent return during the period between age 65 and age 71, her holdings would have grown to over $2 million.

Before reaching age 70½, Holly goes to her accountant for help in determining the best withdrawal method for her to best manage her taxes. Her accountant chooses the "recalculating method." The recalculating method is one of the methods permitted under the tax laws to figure the annual minimum required to be withdrawn from a tax-deferred account. This method refigures her mandatory distributions based on her life expectancy each year. This method of withdrawing funds from a tax-deferred account lengthens the time horizon for withdrawals and lowers current taxes. Using this method, Holly can continue to grow her account while she is withdrawing. If you would like further information on the recalculating method and the term-certain method, I suggest you send for IRS Publication 590, which is available from the IRS by calling 1-800-TAX-FORM.

For purposes of the remaining illustrations, I will raise Holly's effective tax rate to 45 percent after age 65 and lower her investment returns to 6 percent. In comparing her regular account, I will assume that her investments are in tax-free instruments earning a tax-free return of 6 percent. Remember that in order to simplify the calculations in this discussion, I did not increase Holly's salary during her 40 years of employment. Consequently, her preretirement paycheck is $26,000 in these examples. In Appendix A, however, I do show tables that include cost of living adjustments to Holly's compensation throughout her employment, which is a more realistic view of what would happen in her 401(k). I also show different tax scenarios and other changes in the assumptions for your information.

Using the IRS recalculating formula, in her 71st year, Holly will withdraw approximately $150,000 from her $2.3 million

401(k) account, which is the minimum the law requires to be withdrawn. This leaves $2.15 million in her account, which is invested at a 6 percent rate for purposes of our illustration. She will pay taxes of $67,500 on the $150,000 withdrawal at the 45 percent tax rate. (This assumes there is no 15 percent excess tax applicable to the $200,000 withdrawal; the 1996 limit is $155,000.) Her net after-tax withdrawal will be $82,500. During that year, her $2.15 million will have grown at an assumed 6 percent rate to just under $2.3 million.

401(k) Assets at Age 71	$2,300,000
Minimum Withdrawal Required (Recalculating Method)	$150,000
Less Taxes (45%)	−$67,500
After-Tax Withdrawal (Your 401(k) After-Tax Paycheck)	$82,500
Assets Remaining	$2,150,000
Growth of Assets at 6% (Reinvested Tax Deferred in 401(k))	$129,000
Net Assets in 401(k) at the End of the Year	$2,279,000

Each year, Holly will withdraw the minimum amount required by law, based on a percentage of her account value. Because her account continues to grow tax-deferred while she is withdrawing, between the ages of 71 and 91, she will actually be able to withdraw an after-tax pension check of between $80,000 and $100,000 a year into her late 80s. By age 91 she will have withdrawn about $2 million in after-tax "pension" checks, and will have about $500,000 left in her account.

Please remember that the following numbers and those in Appendix A are meant to illustrate the growth potential of a regular versus a 401(k) account, as well as possible withdrawal strategies. Actual results will vary with the markets.

In comparison, using the same assumptions, by age 71, Holly's regular investment account would have grown from $285,000 at age 65 to $395,000 at age 71, having been invested tax-free at 6 percent from age 65 through age 71. From age 71 on, the $375,000 is invested in a 6 percent tax-free investment to give her $22,500 of annual income. Her principal remains at $375,000 throughout her retirement and her after-tax income remains at $22,500 per year.

The following table shows a comparison of the after-tax income withdrawn from the 401(k) to the income withdrawn from the regular account.

AFTER-TAX INCOME WITHDRAWN

	401(k)	REGULAR ACCOUNT
Age 65	$0	$0
Age 71	$82,500	$22,500
Ages 71 Through 91	$2,000,000	$472,500

The following table shows a comparison of the value of the 401(k) account to the value of the regular account for different periods.

VALUE OF CAPITAL

	401(k)	REGULAR ACCOUNT
Age 65	$1,500,000	$285,000
Age 71	$2,300,000	$375,000
Ages 71 Through 91	$2,300,000 to $500,000	$375,000
Age 91	$500,000	$375,000

You can see that the 401(k) assets are being withdrawn from the account over time as you grow older. One of the management issues for individuals using the recalculating method is managing what you do with the funds you withdraw after you pay taxes. In our example, you have much more money than you would need in retirement, based on your preretirement salary. You would need to make arrangements to save the amounts you are paid above and beyond your expense needs for the period beyond the age of 91.

The ability to manage your after-tax income into retirement illustrates the 10th 401(k) advantage, Postretirement Tax Advantages.

These results would be entirely different if Holly had made different choices. Her account would have been much smaller had she chosen a money market fund as her investment, or a contribution level lower than 6 percent. In the case of a money market fund, at retirement, her 401(k) account would have approximated $240,000, compared to $1.5 million to $2 million. Her regular account would have approximated $75,000 instead of $285,000 to $350,000. Had she taken out a loan from her plan and left her employ before repaying it, she might have lowered her 401(k) account balance unnecessarily to repay the loan. In addition, she might have had to pay a 10 percent tax penalty to the IRS for early withdrawal. Also, her results would have been different dramatically if she had started her 401(k) just a few years later. If she waited only five years, her 401(k) account would have grown $500,000 less ($1 million as opposed to $1.5 million).

As you can see, it is of utmost importance that you understand your withdrawal options before you begin taking money out of your 401(k). The choices available to you are determined by the tax code and require a full understanding of the tax law effect of various alternatives. The consequences of choosing one method over another can have a significant impact on your after-tax income throughout retirement. To ensure that you do not forgo tax advantages, be sure to consult your tax attorney or tax accountant well before you begin distributions. Be certain to seek out the assistance of competent tax counsel. The complexity of some of the tax issues involved with withdrawals, spousal rights, estate tax issues, and the like demand the attention of counsel that is well versed in the tax laws affecting 401(k)s.

11

Common 401(k) Mistakes and How to Avoid Them

Perhaps the single most common 401(k) mistake I see is underestimating the great potential and value of your 401(k).

Mistake 1. Deciding not to participate because you don't want your paycheck reduced.

No matter how large or small your paycheck, you may feel you do not have enough to cover all your day-to-day needs. If you are using this excuse not to participate in your 401(k) or to limit your participation to the minimum, you fall into possibly the largest and most luckless mistake category, particularly if your plan provides a company match or profit-sharing contribution. You need to make decisions about buying consumer goods based on your budget. You need to make 401(k) decisions based on your plan.

As you know from reading Chapter 2, there is a difference between a *salary* reduction and a *paycheck* reduction. The 401(k) is a *salary* reduction plan. If you want to minimize your paycheck reduction, work with your human resources department or accountant to figure out how to adjust your tax withholding so that the IRS pays for much of your contribution.

There is absolutely no reason not to participate in a 401(k), since you can do so with a minimum reduction in your paycheck if you adjust your tax withholding. If you are not participating for budgetary reasons, reread Chapter 5, get information about your plan, and rethink your situation. You will find that you can keep your paycheck as high as possible and build a retirement portfolio at the same time. If your plan has a company match or profit-sharing contribution, don't wait until tomorrow, do it now.

Mistake 2. Investing for retirement in a regular account before maximizing your 401(k).

Even if your plan has no company match, your 401(k) puts you far ahead of an investment you might make in a savings or investment account you might set up on your own. The reason you are ahead in your 401(k) is due to its design features, which offer tax advantages and provide an environment in which the potential for compounding your investment is greater than in any regular account you might set up. I explored these design features in Chapter 2, and you may want to review them at this time if you are not participating in your 401(k).

Because of these advantages, the prudent course of action for any successful investor would be to put first things first by maximizing his or her 401(k) before investing for retirement in a regular savings or investment account.

Mistake 3. Not knowing the leverage your plan offers.

If your company has a 401(k) plan that has a company match, then your 401(k) has even greater potential for compounding your investment. As you saw in Chapter 2, 401(k)s with company matches or profit-sharing contributions are the most powerful in terms of the potential for you to grow your assets for retirement. This is due to the operation of all six compounding elements.

These compounding factors have the effect of "leveraging" your investment without your having to take on "margin" risk. As you saw in our illustration[1] in Chapter 2, your paycheck deduc-

---

[1] Assumes a 100 percent company match, and a 25 percent income tax rate, with no effect for FICA taken into account. If you leave the employ of your company before vesting, you will not get the full benefit of the $30 company match.

tion of $22.50 will "buy" you $60 of an investment. Of the $60, $22.50 comes from your paycheck, $7.50 comes from a tax adjustment made by the payroll department, and $30 comes from the company match. The $22.50 and $7.50 are yours to keep no matter what the circumstances, but you will not be able to take them out of the plan until you retire or leave the company.[2] The match is subject to vesting, which in some plans occurs immediately, and in others, occurs in your fifth or seventh year of service with your company, depending on the vesting schedule adopted by your plan. At the latest, by law, your company match must vest when you reach age 65 or complete five years of service if hired after age 60.

Mistake 4. Driving your 401(k) on the highway in low gear for no reason.

Most plans call on you, the participant, to figure out how to maximize the company match. Usually, there is a certain percentage salary contribution that you need to make to trigger the maximum *dollar* contribution from your company. This is the optimal leverage point of your plan as it relates to your paycheck. (If you are a highly compensated employee, you will be limited by tax laws that keep your contribution below legal limits.)

If you don't know your optimal leverage point under your plan, you are probably not putting your 401(k) to full use. If you are doing this, you are giving your 401(k) bonus away, without even knowing how much you are losing. Not knowing your optimal 401(k) leverage point is the most pernicious of the 401(k) mistakes and it can only be attributed to lack of diligence on the employee's part.

You saw in Chapter 5 that finding the optimal leverage point in your plan will mean your account can compound immediately,

---

[2] If you leave the employ of your company before the age of 59½, you will need to roll over the plan into another tax-deferred vehicle, such as an IRA. If you don't you will be subject to penalties and taxes, as discussed in Chapter 3. Other withdrawal possibilities and their limitations are discussed in Chapter 10.

without the assumption of market risk. You could be passing up a bonus of 3, 5, 6, or 10 percent of your yearly salary. Isn't it worth your time to find out if you are?

Mistake 5. Borrowing from the plan for consumer purchases.

One of the selling points used to encourage you to sign up for your 401(k) is that you can borrow money from your plan. The argument goes like this: When you borrow, you are actually borrowing from yourself. As you pay off the loan, you are paying yourself back. When you pay interest on the loan, the interest goes back into your account.

All of this is absolutely true, and for some people in certain cases, a loan from their 401(k) is the only way out of an unforeseen problem. Loan provisions are a blessing in those cases, because if you had to withdraw from your plan prematurely, you would be subject to taxation and a penalty in most cases.

The loan provisions of the 401(k) were never intended to encourage consumer spending. From an investment point of view, it is always a danger to confuse the purpose intended for the investment. I like to see those assets working for you toward your retirement, as opposed to funding current purchases. When you get in the habit of diverting these funds for other purposes, you have to ask yourself how that activity will get you closer to a sufficient retirement asset base for you. You need to keep your priorities straight and be guided by the goal you set out to achieve. Take your retirement planning seriously and think twice before confusing the issue by borrowing to buy consumer goods. And remember, interest on a 401(k) plan loan is rarely tax deductible. Another source, such as a home equity loan, would be more advantageous, that is, tax deductible while preserving your retirement account.

Mistake 6. Selecting investments that have the least chance of growing your assets.

The successful investor always starts with the end in mind. Of the investment options that are presented to you in your plan, some will be better suited for the production of income and some will be better suited for growth of capital.

To be a successful 401(k) investor, you have to understand the difference. If you want to grow your assets, don't pick the investment options that give you the least chance of accomplishing this result.

Mistake 7. Asking your human resources department to tell you what to do with your investments.

Some participants tell me they are not used to investing and find the exercise of making investment selections for their plans overwhelming. If you feel this way, you will not solve the problem by going to your personnel department and asking someone to tell you what to do.

You will be living with your investment results long after you leave the employ of your company. Your human resources professional, no matter how well trained or how well meaning, will not be paying your bills when you are 80.

In order to be successful in your 401(k), you do not need to have exhaustive knowledge of the markets, trading techniques, or years of experience. What you do need is the resolve to learn the basics of your plan and the selection of investment options available to you, and the discipline to stick with a program of investing that is appropriate for your circumstances.

If after reading this book and reviewing your plan literature you need additional assistance, I recommend you and a coworker review the literature together. Sometimes, it helps to be able to talk about what you are reading with someone else. This should get you over the stumbling blocks. If it doesn't, then you owe it to yourself to retain a professional investment adviser to guide you. Expect to pay a fee based on time, not assets.

Mistake 8. Chasing the current top performers.

Some people follow a plan of action that almost guarantees bad results: switching holdings to the current top performer. Top performance figures should never direct your investment activity, whether you are investing in your 401(k) or on your own. You simply don't buy an investment after it has made its move. You buy the investment only if it fits your objective selection criteria and hold it until it is time to make a portfolio change that derives from your portfolio strategy.

Others try to time the market by anticipating when it will go up and when it will go down. Any market-timing systems you might try may work some of the time. I have not seen any that work all of the time. When you are investing for your future, using a crystal ball to guess where the market is going is usually a fruitless effort. It is far better to position yourself in the market and stay the course, until there is a reason to reallocate your portfolio. Following the methodology outlined in Chapter 8 is a much more sound way of investing for the long term. It is far better to participate in the market knowing its volatility characteristics than to invest based on your guess about the direction of the market.

The worst possible way to choose investments for your 401(k) is to buy immediate past performance. The best strategy is to understand your investment options, position yourself appropriately, and stay the course until it is time to reallocate your holdings due to your position in the 401(k) investment life cycle.

Mistake 9. Taking your money out of your 401(k) when you change jobs.

When people change jobs, they may not understand the magnitude of the loss they will suffer by not rolling over their 401(k)s into another tax-deferred vehicle. First, there is an income tax and a tax penalty to be paid. Second, using your retirement assets as spending money may give you immediate satisfaction, but it leaves you behind in building your retirement assets. It is very hard to make up for lost time when it comes to retirement investing. Depending on the circumstances, it may be possible to catch up in certain cases, but only if you have a lot of lead time, invest much more money, and don't hit the legal limits imposed on contributions.

Mistake 10. Looking for a solution in a life cycle fund or an asset allocation fund.

The 401(k) industry has created a fund that is meant to be all things to all people: the life cycle fund or the asset allocation fund. These instruments may be offered as an option in your plan. The problem I see with these funds is that any time you have a one-size-fits-all solution, you tend to get a baggy fit.

It is far better for you to make your investment selections based on where you are in your 401(k) cycle, instead of where everyone else is.

The next chapter deals with special issues you may come across, including more information on taxation of distributions.

12

Special Issues

In other chapters, I explored the contribution, investment, and withdrawal decisions you will be called upon to make in your 401(k). In this chapter, I will look a little more closely at pretax versus after-tax contributions and discuss withdrawals, enrollment forms, and account statements. I will explore additional decisions you may need to make in certain special cases such as changing jobs, disability, estate planning, divorce, or bankruptcy. I will also touch on special issues that relate to your 401(k) if you are one of your company's more highly compensated employees. Finally, I will refer you to sources of additional information.

PRETAX VERSUS AFTER-TAX ACCOUNTS

Many times I see 401(k) enrollment forms that allow you to choose to contribute to your plan on a pretax or after-tax basis, or both, with no added information given on the significance of the choices. The tax laws limit the amount you can contribute pretax to $9,500, as of 1996. This maximum is increased periodically by the IRS. If you are at or near the limit, you may wish to check with your human resources department to determine the current maximum. If you are a highly compensated employee, your maximum contribution may be limited to a *lower* amount by IRS rules prohibiting discrimination in favor of highly compensated employees.

There is no Pretax Advantage on amounts contributed after-tax. However, you do benefit from Tax-Deferred Growth and the Reinvestment Privilege. Consequently, after you have contributed the maximum permissible on a pretax basis, it may be advantageous for you to contribute after-tax. If you have any questions about the maximum pretax contributions you can make, your human resources department will give you the information you need to take full advantage of pretax contributions before beginning after-tax contributions.

WITHDRAWALS OR DISTRIBUTIONS

By law, you may receive a complete distribution from your 401(k) plan at retirement, death, disability, reaching the age of 59½, or termination of your employment. You have some options in how to receive payment, each of which has consequences that need to be fully understood beforehand. Certain plans also permit "hardship withdrawals" during your employment for medical expenses, for tuition payments, or to purchase a principal residence. In order to obtain a hardship withdrawal from your plan, you need to demonstrate the need and support it with documentation. If you receive a hardship withdrawal or disability payment, both are subject to withholding and taxation.

The early withdrawal penalty is not applicable under any circumstances if you are 59½ years of age or older, or if you die, regardless of age at the date of death. There are a few instances in which the penalty does not apply under the age of 59½, such as disability. However, you will have to check with your plan administrator to make certain. In addition, if you separate from service from your employer, you are exempt from the penalty if you are 55 or older (not 59½).

If you receive payment in one lump sum, your pretax account, your company contribution account, and all plan earnings will be subject to 20 percent withholding and income taxes, and if you receive payment before the age of 59½, you may be subject to the

10 percent early withdrawal penalty. Any amounts that you contributed to your 401(k) on an after-tax basis would not be subject to taxation or withholding, since you have already paid income taxes on these amounts. Likewise, you would not be able to roll over these amounts into an IRA.

Normally, all of the distribution will be eligible for rollover to another tax-deferred account in order to continue tax-deferral benefits, except for contributions you made to your after-tax account.

You can receive a distribution in a single payment or "lump sum." It is usually possible to receive your distribution over time, as well, in the form of annuity payments over (1) your lifetime or (2) your lifetime and the lifetime of your spouse or other beneficiary. If you take the lump-sum distribution, you are eligible to continue the benefits of tax deferral by rolling over or transferring your account into a new IRA you set up with your broker, banker, investment adviser, or mutual fund for that purpose. You can arrange to have your lump-sum distribution rolled directly into your new IRA by directing your employer based upon instructions from the receiving IRA custodian. If you do not arrange a direct transfer, you will receive your lump-sum distribution in a check with 20 percent deducted for withholding taxes. To continue tax-deferral benefits, you will need to deposit the check with your IRA custodian before you lose the option to do so, which is 60 days after you receive payment. You will need to add an amount equal to the 20 percent withheld for taxes or that 20 percent will be considered a taxable distribution. The money you roll over will not be taxed until distribution, which must begin at the age of 70½.

If you do not roll over, but wish to keep your lump-sum distribution and pay taxes on it, and you are 59½ or older, "five-year averaging," which is a one-time special tax treatment, may lower your taxes. If you elect to use five-year averaging, your taxes will equal five times the tax payable on one-fifth of your distribution, probably at a lower tax rate. There have been proposals to eliminate the five-year averaging election. As with all distribution options, be certain to check with your tax lawyer or tax accountant to determine appropriate tax alternatives for your particular situation, well before your planned distribution.

ENROLLMENT FORMS

The best enrollment forms allow you to see the impact your salary reduction will have on your paycheck and the benefits of participating. A good example is the XYZ Group enrollment form provided in Appendix B, which is personalized for each eligible employee. In this example, John is 40 years old. His salary is $70,000 a year, and his company match is 100 percent with a cap of 6 percent of salary. His plan allows him to contribute 2 percent to 12 percent of salary.

If you were John, you would be able to quickly assess the benefits of immediate compounding at the different salary contribution levels permitted by the plan at your salary. You would see that if you contributed 6 percent, your $51.38 paycheck reduction (line 2 of section 1 of the enrollment form) would "buy" you $161.54 of 401(k) assets (line 5), for a net immediate gain of $110.16 (line 6), before investments. You would be able to compare what a $25.69 paycheck reduction (3 percent contribution) would "buy" you ($80.76), with a net immediate gain of $55.07. With this information, you could make a reasoned decision. Between these two options, which would you choose?

Enrollment forms of this type are most useful, since they show you the benefits of immediate compounding as they relate to your particular situation, factoring in the Leveraged Paycheck (line 2), the Pretax Advantage (line 3) and the Match Advantage (line 4).

Another interesting aspect of the enrollment form is section 3, which shows that if you wait five years to begin participating, it will cost you. At the 6 percent contribution level, you can see that you would be $415,192 behind when you retire, simply by waiting five years to begin participating. If your firm does not provide such enrollment forms, you can make these calculations on your own with the help of your human resources department.

Account Statements

As a participant in your 401(k), you will receive statements of account from your plan administrator that show you the status of your account at the end of each calendar quarter. There is quite a bit of variety in terms of the amount and nature of information provided on statements.

The best statements provide you with two types of information: details on transactions and a summary of plan activity.

Transaction detail should include the date upon which your payroll deduction and company matches are deposited in your 401(k) account, the amount of your beginning balance, the payroll contribution in dollars, how the money is invested (including the purchase price per share, number of shares purchased, total shares held, purchased, or sold during the period, and dividends and capital gains reinvested during the period), and total value of the account.

With this information, you can follow the movement of funds into your account and track your performance. Some statements also show your results compared to appropriate benchmarks, such as the S&P, as well as a summary or graphic depiction of the composition of your portfolio.

The statement should summarize activity in each of your 401(k) accounts, pretax, after-tax, and employer match (and employer profit sharing). The beginning balance of each account should be shown, along with the individual holdings of each account, contributions made during the period, loan repayments, investment earnings, distributions, transfers, forfeitures, dollar balance at the end of the period, and vested balance at the end of the period. An example of a statement is provided in Appendix B. The first two pages of the statement contain the plan summary and the next several pages contain the transaction detail.

When you receive your statement, you should review it to ascertain that all funds expected posted accurately. In addition, check your investment allocations for accuracy.

Usually, your statement will be accompanied by a quarterly

performance report listing all the investment alternatives provided by your plan and "total returns" for the last year, 5 years, and 10 years or the life of the fund, if less than 10 years. Total return is a number calculated to show (1) the change in "net asset value" from the beginning of the period to the end of the period and (2) the dividends and capital gains paid per share during the period. Net asset value (NAV) is basically the price per share of the fund.

The underlying assumption to the total return calculation is that dividends and capital gains are reinvested. Accordingly, if you were withdrawing dividends during the distribution stage of your 401(k), the total return would be less meaningful to you than if you were reinvesting dividends during your accumulation phase. Total return can be shown in two forms, "cumulative" and "annualized."

Cumulative return is a number that reflects the difference between a beginning value and ending value over some period of years. The annualized return is the average annual compounded rate of return on an investment made at the beginning of the period and held through the end of the period. For example, you may see a fund as having a cumulative return of 400.65 percent cumulative and 17.48 percent annualized.

These numbers are significant only for purposes of comparing the past returns of alternative investments, which in large part reflect the state of the markets during the time period chosen. They do not give you any indication of risk, volatility, or potential return. When you get the performance statement be especially careful of any urge to switch your holdings based on the numbers. Instead, make your investment selections based on your long-term strategy in light of where you are in your 401(k) life cycle.

CHANGING JOBS

If you are contemplating changing jobs, there are three important 401(k) issues for you to understand well in advance of your leaving your present employer. You will have some decisions to make, depending on how your plan deals with these issues. Making the wrong choices can mean early withdrawal penalties, additional taxes, and lost opportunity. These issues are (1) outstanding loans, if any, (2) vesting, and (3) required distributions.

Outstanding Loans. Depending on the provisions of your plan, you may suffer severe consequences if you have any outstanding loans at the time you leave your employ. Some plans provide that if you cannot repay the loan when you terminate employment, you will be deemed to have defaulted on your loan and your company will exercise its right to deduct the amount of your loan from any distribution you would receive when you leave. Should this occur, your default (and the company's subsequent exercise of its security interest on the loan) is deemed a "distribution" by the IRS, subjecting you to (a) the 10 percent early withdrawal penalty if you are under the age of 55 (not 59½) and (b) income taxes on the amount of the loan if you borrowed from your pretax account.

You should explore whether your plan allows you to transfer your loan to your new employer's plan, and whether the new employer's plan allows you to roll over an existing loan. This might be a good option for you to consider, since you will be able to continue paying off the loan while you are working in your new job and maintain your full retirement savings despite your job change. If not, consider seeking cash from other sources to pay off the loan to preserve your retirement savings via rollover into a new plan or IRA. A possible source of cash is a tax-deductible home equity loan.

Vesting. You need to assure yourself that you are vested in your company match or profit-sharing contributions, since you will not be able to take unvested portions with you if you leave. If you are short of vesting time, you might reconsider your decision to leave your company until you are fully vested. You should also ask about break in service rules under your plan, which allow you to pick up on your years of service if you return to your company after having left.

Required Distributions. It is possible that your plan may mandate your 401(k) assets be paid or "distributed" to you when you leave the employ of the company. Any time you have a distribution out of your account, you have to consider the loss of deferral opportunities, tax consequences, and tax penalties that apply and ways to avoid them. In the case of severance of employment, IRS early withdrawal penalties apply only if you are under the age of 55 (instead of 59½). Distribution checks are reduced by 20 percent for withholding taxes and by the amount of any outstanding loan balances.

To avoid these consequences, most individuals opt to transfer or "roll over" their 401(k) assets into another tax-deferred account. They may choose to transfer to the 401(k) of their new employer, assuming the new employer's plan accepts transfers. Or they may choose to roll over their assets directly into a new IRA set up specifically for the purpose of receiving their 401(k) assets. It is often better to roll over to a new IRA, not an existing IRA, as this preserves the ability to roll over to another qualified plan in the future.

In either case, you would not want to have your current employer give you a distribution check from your 401(k), because it would be reduced by 20 percent withholding. Instead, you should provide transfer instructions supplied by the new employer or IRA custodian to the company you are leaving, and the transfer will be done without withholding. If you do receive a check, it will be for only 80 percent of your account with 20 percent withheld for income-tax purposes.

You should be certain to take action within the 60-day grace period the IRS gives you to roll over this money (plus the amount withheld) into another tax-deferred account. If you roll over only the amount you received by check, which is 80 percent of your account value, the 20 percent withheld will be considered a distribution subject to taxes and early withdrawal penalties. The tax laws permit you to substitute other money to replace the amount withheld, in order to avoid taxes and penalties on the amount withheld.

If you miss the 60-day grace period by even one day with respect to all or any portion of the distribution, you will be considered to have taken a taxable distribution in the amount not rolled over. There are no extensions available beyond the 60-day period.

If you opt for a transfer into a new IRA, you should secure rollover forms from your broker, banker, or mutual fund family and provide them to your current employer. These forms will instruct your employer to transfer your assets in full to your new IRA directly. This procedure avoids the need for 20 percent withholding for taxes. The transfer most likely will be made in cash, which means that all your 401(k) holdings will be liquidated at the time of the instruction. In the alternative, it may be possible for you to direct your holdings to be transferred "in kind." This means that your holdings will not be sold, but merely transferred onto the books of the new trustee or custodian. Your shares of Mutual Fund XYZ held in your 401(k) would be moved into your rollover IRA account at the mutual fund or brokerage firm of your choice.

Usually, plans must give you an additional option: keeping your assets with the employer you are leaving. Before making a decision on what to do, you will need to see if your new employer provides a 401(k) that permits you to transfer your previous employer's 401(k) assets and to compare the provisions of the two plans, as well as the pros and cons of setting up an IRA rollover.

DISABILITY

Plans typically allow you to withdraw from them if you become disabled, and your disability is deemed termination of service for purposes of the withdrawal. "Disability" is defined in your plan. Generally, you are disabled if you are unable to engage in any substantial gainful activity for the foreseeable future. If you get a distribution from your plan due to disability, you are subject to income tax, but not the 10 percent early withdrawal penalty, and your check will be reduced by 20 percent for withholding.

ESTATE PLANNING

After your death, your pretax account, your after-tax account, and your vested employer contributions are paid out to your beneficiary, less loan balances and forfeitures. Early withdrawal penalties do not apply in the case of death.

You need to be aware of three types of taxes that apply and factor them into your overall estate plan. First, an income tax would be due on the full amount of the distribution to your beneficiary, when received, taxable at the beneficiary's tax rate as income. The date of receipt may be delayed by the beneficiary for up to five years, thus delaying income tax liability, if you die before the age of 70½. If you die between the ages of 59½ and 70½, your beneficiary may take the distribution in full at your death, but spread out income tax liability over five years through the special one-time five-year income-averaging election, which can effectively lower overall taxes on the distribution. No matter what your age at the date of death, if you designate a natural person (not your estate, a charity, or a revocable trust) as beneficiary, your beneficiary may elect to receive distributions over his or her lifetime as determined by actuarial tables published by the IRS.

Special tax rules apply if the beneficiary is the surviving spouse. He or she will have the option of rolling over the 401(k) into his or her IRA to continue tax deferral. If he or she takes a distribution, either in a lump sum or in periodic payments, the distribution will be fully taxable as income at the beneficiary's tax rates when received. Five-year averaging (discussed under "Withdrawals or Distributions," above) may be available to the surviving spouse in certain circumstances. A nonspouse beneficiary is taxed on any distribution from the plan when received, whether paid in a lump sum, annuity, or installment payments.

The treatment of 401(k)s and other tax-deferred accounts under the tax laws governing estates is complex and calls for special expertise and planning. Generally, your 401(k) assets are included in your gross estate and subject to federal and state estate and succession taxes. Perhaps the most important estate-planning issue is the designation of a beneficiary of your 401(k) assets, which is something you do when you first begin participating in your 401(k). If you designate your spouse as the beneficiary of your 401(k), the estate tax marital deduction is generally available so that 401(k) benefits are not subject to estate and succession taxes. As discussed above, depending on their situation, some individuals designate as beneficiaries their children, grandchildren, a trust, or a charity (but not their estate).

Receiving competent counsel from a trusts and estates attorney regarding your 401(k) is especially important if your 401(k) assets are substantial, or comprise a substantial part of your estate. For example, you need to factor into your overall planning the excess accumulations tax of 15 percent that may be imposed on your estate. This is a tax that is in addition to any income tax or estate or succession tax that might be due and payable. Whether tax is due depends on a valuation of the account at the date of death based on an IRS formula that takes into account a hypothetical life annuity and the age of the decedent and may also depend on whether your surviving spouse is the beneficiary of your 401(k) assets. The effect of the excess accumulations tax can be lessened with effective tax planning or the creation of an insurance trust to pay the tax.

If you have a large estate, there are additional estate-planning issues. When you speak to your lawyer about your will and estate planning, be sure to interview him or her about experience with tax-deferred plans generally, and about 401(k)s specifically. You need counsel who fully appreciates the complexity of the tax law treatment of tax-deferred accounts to guide you in your estate planning, as well as your withdrawal strategy after you retire. With effective tax planning, you can take advantage of the various ways the tax laws allow you to lower taxes and avoid penalties.

SPOUSAL RIGHTS

By law, your spouse has certain rights in your plan that you cannot give up without his or her consent. Your plan may require all distributions to be paid to you in annuity form, with survivor annuity benefits payable to your surviving spouse, unless you waive your right to that form of payment and your spouse consents in writing to the waiver. Similarly, your spouse's consent may be necessary for a loan. Even if your plan does not generally require survivor annuity benefits, by law, your plan must provide a spousal death benefit that cannot be waived without your spouse's written consent.

DIVORCE

A court may issue a domestic relations order known as a "QDRO" that provides for the payment of child support, alimony, or division of marital property. A QDRO can direct all or a portion of your 401(k) assets to be paid to your spouse or former spouse, child, or other dependent. Absent a QDRO, your plan administrator cannot pay your 401(k) assets to anyone other than you or your named beneficiary upon your death. You will be subject to income taxes on payments pursuant to a QDRO that are not made to your spouse or former spouse. The 10 percent penalty tax on premature distributions does *not* apply to payments made under a QDRO.

BANKRUPTCY

If you file for bankruptcy, your undistributed 401(k) assets cannot be reached by your creditors. If you have a loan outstanding from your 401(k) plan while you are in bankruptcy, your plan administrator may be required to cease collection efforts, including repayment through payroll deduction. Bankruptcy does not, however, affect the rule that a default on a loan will cause the loan to be treated as a distribution to you, subject to income tax and the 10 percent tax penalty for early withdrawals.

Special Issues for the Highly Compensated

Special tax rules limit the amount a "highly compensated employee" can defer into his or her 401(k). Generally, you are classified as a highly compensated employee for 1996 if you: (1) are a 5 percent owner of your employer; (2) receive compensation over $100,000; (3) receive compensation over $66,000 and you are among the highest-paid 20 percent of employees; or (4) are an officer and receive compensation in excess of $60,000. Congress has been considering simplifying the definition of highly compensated employee to include only 5 percent owners and persons receiving compensation over $80,000.

These tax rules limit amounts highly compensated employees can contribute to their plans each year and the total amount, including both the employee pretax and the employer matching contributions, that can be added to the 401(k) accounts of a highly compensated employee. Two IRS tests are applied to determine maximum permitted contributions, the elective deferral limit ($9,500 in 1996), which applies to all participants regardless of compensation, and section 415 limits (the lesser of $30,000 or 25 percent of compensation).

You may want to consider using the amount you would have contributed but for this limitation to make after-tax contributions to your 401(k), which would at least preserve the compounding benefits of Tax-Deferred Growth and the Reinvestment Privilege. To illustrate the combined effect of the two limits, and the possible interplay between pretax and after-tax contributions, let's look at an individual earning $240,000 contributing 9 percent of his salary to a 401(k) with a 66.6 percent company match on his pretax deferrals, capping at 6 percent of salary. Only $150,000 salary can be used for the calculations, due to limits imposed by the tax laws. At 9 percent of $150,000 (not $240,000), the annual contribution would be $13,500 ($1,125 per month), which is above the elective deferral limit of $9,500 for 1996.

Each month, the employee's elective contribution would be $1,125 and his match would be $750. By September, he will have reached the limit of $9,500 pretax contribution, at which time his salary reduction would go into his after-tax account for the remainder of the year. At the same time, his pretax, after-tax, and match contributions are cumulating for purposes of section 415 limits. At year end, his company match account totals $6,333 and he has $9,500 in his pretax account, both of which are controlled by the deferral limit, and $4,000 in his after-tax account. (None of these figures include the results of his investments.) A table is provided in Appendix C showing the monthly calculations, should you wish to follow them.

If your pretax contribution in any year exceeds the applicable tax limits, the excess is paid back to you by the plan. These amounts will be subject to income tax, but no early withdrawal penalty.

As noted earlier, *distributions* in excess of a specified dollar amount each year ($155,000 in 1996) are subject to a 15 percent tax on the portion withdrawn above that amount. Thus, you should assess your situation well before required minimum distributions begin at age 70½ to minimize or avoid this tax.

SOURCES OF ADDITIONAL INFORMATION

As you can see from the above discussion, your rights to your 401(k) assets might be affected by your personal plans. When in doubt about what your particular plan provides, consult your 401(k) summary plan description, or SPD, which is part of the enrollment package. The SPD is a document prepared by your employer pursuant to requirements under law summarizing all the important elements of your plan. A more detailed plan document is filed with the IRS and is available to you to review upon request.

In addition to the issues discussed above, the SPD covers eligibility, matching, the definition of compensation for purposes of the plan, the definition of disability and normal retirement dates, death benefits for beneficiaries, vesting, forfeitures, termination of employment, rollovers from other plans, fund administration and valuation of assets, lump-sum distributions, in-service distributions, loans, forfeitures, taxes on contributions and distributions. Your company may also provide special brochures on distributions, loans, and hardship withdrawals, in addition to forms you will need to fill out related to these plan features. In addition, your employer or plan administrator generally must provide you, at least 30 days and not more than 90 days before you receive a distribution, a tax disclosure statement outlining your rollover rights and other tax information. You may also wish to call the IRS to ask for IRS Publication 590 on IRAs, which deals with issues you will need to understand if you do a rollover, and IRS Publication 575 on Pension and Annuity Income, which governs taxation of distributions from 401(k)s and other tax-deferred accounts.

If you would like information about mutual funds, which are the investment of choice of many 401(k) plans, you may write or call the Investment Company Institute for a catalog of publications. These educational booklets are especially helpful to the novice investor. I highly recommend "An Investor's Guide to Reading the Mutual Fund Prospectus," which takes you through each section of a prospectus, defining terms and helping you put in perspective the information you may find in different types of offerings. Two other good publications are "What is a Mutual Fund?" and "Directory of Mutual Funds." Both booklets are available by calling or writing the ICI, which is located at 1401 H Street, NW, Washington, DC 20005. Telephone: (202) 326-5872.

13

Your Rights and Responsibilities as a 401(k) Participant

YOUR RIGHTS

You are the beneficiary of certain protections afforded 401(k) participants by law. Most of your rights will be referred to in your summary plan document, which is required to be given to you by your employer when you enroll in your plan.

To protect against any potential loss of your 401(k) due to claims of your employer's creditors, your contributions and those of all other employees in your plan are required to be segregated from your company's funds. Your funds are held for you in trust by the plan's trustee. Thus, your 401(k) assets are protected in the event of the failure of your company's business or bankruptcy. This does not mean, however, that your company's stock price won't go down in value, which in turn will affect your 401(k) if you own company stock in the account.

To protect against your employer acting in its own self-interest with your retirement assets, the law places the high legal standard of a "fiduciary" on your employer. A fiduciary assumes a position of trust, acting in the interest of the beneficiaries of your plan — you and your fellow 401(k) plan participants. Your employer's fiduciary duty is federally mandated by the Employee Retirement Income Security Act of 1974 (ERISA) and extends to all aspects of the operation of your plan.

In the exercise of its fiduciary responsibility, your employer should carefully screen the initial investment offerings of your

plan and review them periodically to ensure the selection continues to be suitable for the plan's participants. Your employer,
through the plan's administrator, should provide you accurate and
current information about your investment options and invest your
payroll deductions and company contribution on a timely basis.

With self-directed 401(k)s, which are the subject of this book,
you have the right to choose your investments from the selection
offered and to change your holdings from time to time, as well as
the amounts you contribute. The circumstances under which you
can make changes are governed by the provisions of your plan.

Your summary plan description or other plan literature will give
you the guidelines that apply in your case. Some companies
provide a calendar setting out how you can make changes and the
date the changes will become effective. For example, you might
find if you submit a request to change your rate of contribution (or
a request to suspend your contributions) during the first two weeks
of the month, the change will be effective the first of the following
month. If you want to take out a loan, the calendar might provide
that if you make your request between the 1st and the 15th of the
month, you will receive a check the last business day of the
month. If you make the request after the 15th, you will receive
the check on the 15th of the following month, and so on.

You might find that if you want to change your investment
instructions, you can make the request any day of the month, to be
effective the following pay period. If you want to sell one of your
holdings to buy another, you might find you can do so any business
day of the month, with the transaction being effective the next day.

In contrast to a traditional pension plan that your company
might offer, you have the right to take your 401(k) pretax and
after-tax accounts with you when you change jobs. Whether you
can take your employer's matching or profit-sharing contributions
with you will depend on whether you are vested in accordance
with the provisions of your plan. Your plan might provide for
immediate vesting, in which case you can take your entire account, including company contributions, with you. In other cases,
your plan will set out a vesting schedule.

Vesting schedules provide for a certain period of employment with the company, regardless of how long you have been participating in the plan. One plan, for example, provides that if you work there for more than three but fewer than four years, you will be 60 percent vested in your company match. If your plan has a comparable provision and you leave during your fourth year of service, you will be able to take with you 60 percent of your company match account as well as 100 percent of your employee account, whether it is pretax or after-tax, and 100 percent of your rollover account, if you rolled over money into your 401(k) when you joined the company.

Under current law, a company may not extend a vesting schedule beyond seven years. If you have worked for your company for more than seven years, you should be 100 percent vested in all of your 401(k) account, including company contributions. In the event you leave the employ of your company and return within a certain period of time specified in your plan, generally, you have a right to receive credit for the time you were previously employed with the company.

In certain very limited cases, you have a right to withdraw funds from your account while you are still employed. These cases are described in your summary plan document. For example, some companies permit withdrawals in cases of disability and some do not. Some plans provide loans and some do not. You will have to refer to your company's plan to determine whether your plan provides this options.

If your plan permits, you may be able to withdraw funds from your vested account for demonstrated "financial hardship." Typically, you would be able to withdraw by showing a heavy financial need for medical bills, college tuition, or the purchase of your home, or any other financial need determined to be a hardship by the plan administrator. The withdrawals permitted typically include the amount needed to cover the particular hardship, as well as the income taxes and early withdrawal tax penalty that would be due on the sums at withdrawal.

You have the right to borrow from your account only if your

plan has loan provisions. If it does, the plan usually limits the amount of the loan to one-half of your vested balance or $50,000, whichever is less, so that the loan will not be deemed a "distribution" for tax purposes. You will have to sign a note promising to repay the loan. The promissory note will be payable to the trustee of the plan. The note will specify an interest rate and term, which is generally not more than five years unless the loan is used to acquire your principal residence. The note will specify that the interest and principal payments must be made at least quarterly in substantially equal amounts. Normally, payments are made automatically through payroll deductions.

If you become disabled, some plans allow you to withdraw from the plan under the provisions dealing with regular withdrawals. However, in such cases, your withdrawals are still subject to income taxes and, in some cases, early withdrawal penalties if you are under 59½.

Whether you have a right to leave your 401(k) intact after you retire will depend on the plan. Some plans provide for mandatory distributions when you leave the company at normal retirement age. Some plans permit you to maintain the account intact until age 70½ when required minimum distributions begin. However, even those plans require a full mandatory distribution at severance if your account is worth $3,500 or less.

You have a right to designate a beneficiary who would receive the vested portion of your account. Your plan will provide what happens if you do not designate a beneficiary or if your designation is invalid for any reason. If you are married and wish to designate someone other than your spouse, your spouse must give written consent to the designation of another beneficiary. There are different rules governing distributions to beneficiaries depending on whether and how you handle your beneficiary designation. When distributions might begin differs, as well as the treatment of distributions for income and estate tax purposes, which are issues beyond the scope of this book. I recommend that you discuss these issues with your tax adviser.

If you have a disagreement with your plan's administrator about

Your Rights and Responsibilities as a 401(k) Participant   159

any benefits that you believe might be due to you, you have the right to present your point of view for review by the administrator in accordance with the procedures set out in your plan. By law, every 401(k) plan must provide for review procedures. After exhausting your appeals with your administrator, if you wish to pursue your claim further, your final recourse is with the Department of Labor or the federal courts, depending on the nature of your grievance.

YOUR RESPONSIBILITIES

Unlike a traditional pension program in which an employee is a passive participant, a self-directed 401(k) requires active involvement on your part. It is your responsibility to put your 401(k) to good use.

If you decide not to contribute to the plan, you might find yourself without sufficient assets to live on after you retire. If you decide to participate but are not diligent in directing your investment selections, you may suffer a similar result. If you fail to understand how to maximize the company match in your plan, when you are 75 or 80 you might wonder how your former coworkers can afford to live so much better than you.

Whether you can successfully pursue a legal claim against your employer when you are 80 years old and out of money is not my focus here. If you are reading this book, I assume that you want to take charge of your future. Accordingly, in the following discussion, I am dealing not with legal issues but with issues of self-determination and responsibility for your own well-being.

It is folly to think that your human resources department, boss, or coworker has the investment expertise or knowledge of your personal finances necessary to make your investment selections for you. It is your responsibility to fully understand your investment, contribution, and withdrawal options as well as the issues relating to tax management when you or your beneficiary begins withdrawing from your 401(k).

If you can read this book, you can read the plan documents, prospectuses, and financial reports provided by your employer to help you make reasoned choices. This is not a formidable task. It is a matter of gathering current materials and focusing on the issues initially and returning to them periodically. This seems to be a fair price to pay considering the potential payoffs. After the 401(k) is in place, it is a matter of following your investments and monitoring your results against your objectives and against benchmarks you set for yourself.

In addition to investment selection, it is your responsibility to know how you can lower the market risk of your account by diversifying your holdings. No matter how well-managed and successful your company and how familiar you are with it, investing a large part or all of your account in your company stock creates a risk you do not want to assume. If your match or profit-sharing contribution is paid in company stock, you need to be sure to invest your own contributions in a diversified portfolio.

When you consider changing jobs, it is your responsibility to make certain that you understand how much of your 401(k) you can take with you, which is a question of vesting. In addition, you need to know how any outstanding loans will be treated under the plan, and the consequences of taking a distribution and spending the money. With this information, you will not lose tax-deferred money or inadvertently subject yourself to taxes and penalties.

Don't make the mistake of using a job change as an opportunity to spend your 401(k) money. Instead, continue your tax-deferral benefits by keeping your 401(k), or rolling it over into an IRA of your choice or your new employer's 401(k), should transfer options be available. If you fail to do a rollover within 60 days of distribution, no extensions are available to you and you will have to pay income taxes and early withdrawal penalties, if applicable.

It is your responsibility to make sure you receive competent tax advice before you begin to make withdrawals from your account. There are a number of withdrawal options available to you as a 401(k) participant, and you will not be able to hold anyone responsible for paying taxes or penalties you could have avoided with adequate tax counsel. You need to find a tax accountant or tax lawyer who is specially trained in retirement-plan distributions and estate planning, particularly if you have a large 401(k) account or large estate. You need to begin interviewing prospective tax advisers well before retirement to be certain that you find someone who understands the issues and is able to work with you and your investment adviser to plan your distribution and disposition strategy in a tax-advantaged manner.

This is not meant as an exhaustive review of rights and responsibilities, but one that will get you to think ahead before setting out on a course that may have some undesirable consequences. As you work with your 401(k) plan options and understand the flexibility and limitations of your own plan, you will see more and more of the alternatives your 401(k) can provide you. As you go forward, keep in mind your responsibilities as a 401(k) investor to more fully enjoy the many benefits your 401(k) offers.

14

Where to Go from Here

The starting point for you as a participant is to make certain you have all the materials you need to manage your 401(k) investment portfolio. Before making any decisions, make sure that your 401(k) packet contains *current and complete* information about all of your investment choices. From time to time, I see out of date materials that do not reflect options currently available and packages that are missing key information. While it is the legal obligation of the company to provide current and complete information, if you have any doubts about your package, double-check everything before you start making decisions.

Any time one of your options is a mutual fund or annuity, you need to see a prospectus to understand the nature of what is being offered. Prospectuses are legal documents written for the protection of investors. They follow a formula set out by the federal securities laws and are intended to disclose to investors all the risks they need to be apprised of before they invest.

The way to read prospectuses or other investment disclosures is to lay them out next to each other and compare one to another. As you become familiar with the way in which prospectuses are written, you will be able to find information that will be useful to you. For example, by comparing investment objectives and risks, you will be able to distinguish each offering based on whether and how you might use it in your portfolio. As you become more adept at using the investment tools available to you, you will gain in experience and develop the very important skill of managing your own money.

With a well-developed 401(k) portfolio strategy, you will be able to stay on course and rebalance your portfolio as needed. With an awareness of the dangers, you will be better prepared to deal with them.

No matter how disciplined you are about following your investment strategy, you have to anticipate and avoid any tendency to stray from course. One of the most dangerous times will be when your current performance figures arrive in the mail.

In a rising market, your performance reports will show some investments outperforming others. If you are an inexperienced investor you might be tempted to switch your holdings to the current top performer. In a down market, you will see some investments retaining their market value and others falling. You might be tempted to sell your "losing" holdings in favor of a higher performer or to switch to a money market fund or guaranteed investment contract that is stable in price. Chasing performance in this manner is a good way to lock in losses, miss market moves, and lower the overall performance of your 401(k) portfolio.

More seasoned investors would look at current performance figures to assess whether an investment is acting as expected. You should be able to rely on your company to be doing this sort of assessment for you on a continuing basis in the execution of its fiduciary responsibilities in respect of the plan.

To illustrate, let's say an S&P Index fund drops sharply when the S&P Index itself is flat. This is an indication of a problem, just as much as a 30 percent rise when the S&P Index is up 20 percent. A growth and income fund that outperforms the broad market by a significant amount may be using enhancement techniques such as options trading, futures, leveraging, or the like, or may be weighting certain sectors more heavily than others. These portfolio techniques might increase the risk of the fund beyond expectations.

When I counsel clients with respect to their 401(k) investments, current performance is only one factor I consider to assess the investment vehicle, and as you can see from the discussion, what I am looking for will probably be different from what you might be looking for. What is more important to me as an adviser is the nature of the investment vehicle in terms of investment policies, limitations and style, other options available, and, most important, consistency of performance against objectives.

As 401(k) investors, it is not your job to find the most recent best performer on your menu of investment selections. Your job is to achieve your long-term objective of having enough money to live on retirement. When you feel the urge to stray from your strategy due to current performance figures, always be sure to understand your motivation. Fear and greed are not appropriate motivators when it comes to 401(k) investing, as 401(k) investing is a long-term enterprise. Selling into a falling market will not move you forward. Neither will chasing the current top performers. Sticking to your basic 401(k) life cycle strategy of investing is much more likely to get you to where you want to go, even though your investment choices will not always be at the top of the charts in terms of performance.

You may be starting out with limited investment experience. In the beginning, you may not even know what questions to ask. Your expertise as a 401(k) investor will evolve as you evolve. Later, as you study your investment materials and array and assess your options, you will start to see the risk/reward tradeoffs and how they might affect you. As you develop your strategy for your position in the 401(k) life cycle, you will see how the various options available to you might fit in your plan.

As you implement your strategy you will begin to see your account grow due to your contributions, your company contributions, and the effect of the 401(k)'s six compounding elements. In good market periods, you will see your account increase in market value. In bad market periods, you will see decreases in market value. As you gain in experience, the wisdom of staying within your life cycle strategy will become apparent to you.

Unlike other generations of workers, in many cases, you will not have a traditional company pension to rely on for income in retirement and Social Security may provide only a fraction of what you will need. You may have retired friends or relatives who need to supplement their pension and Social Security income with their personal savings. Projecting into the future, it is reasonable to assume that you and future generations will need to turn to their personal savings and 401(k)s as their *primary* sources of retirement income.

You and other 401(k) participants are discovering that you need to take charge of your future. Companies need to provide appropriate investment selections and reliable, current, and well-articulated information that will help you array your options in a logical manner. These two elements, (1) a suitable investment selection and (2) adequate information to enable you, the employee, to distinguish your options, are essential to your ability to build your retirement assets. It is up to your company to provide these tools and it is up to you, the participant, to put them to good use. At stake is your ability to support yourself when you are no longer working.

You and your 401(k) will be together for a long time, at least as long as you are working and possibly 20 or 30 years or more into your retirement. If you pay some attention to it now, your 401(k) will take care of you for the rest of your life.

Glossary: Types of Mutual Funds

SOURCE: 1995–1996 DIRECTORY OF MUTUAL FUNDS,
PUBLISHED BY THE INVESTMENT COMPANY INSTITUTE[1]

Aggressive Growth Funds seek maximum capital gains as their investment objective. Current income is not a significant factor. Some may invest in stocks of businesses that are somewhat out of the mainstream, such as fledgling companies, new industries, companies fallen on hard times, or industries temporarily out of favor. Some may also use specialized investment techniques such as option writing or short-term trading.

Balanced Funds generally have a three-part investment objective: (1) to conserve investors' initial principal, (2) to pay current income, and (3) to promote long-term growth of both principal and income. Balanced funds have a portfolio mix of bonds, preferred stocks, and common stocks.

Corporate Bond Funds seek a high level of income by purchasing bonds of corporations for the majority of the fund's portfolio. The rest of the portfolio may be in U.S. Treasury bonds or bonds issued by a federal agency.

Flexible Portfolio Funds may be 100 percent invested in stocks *or* bonds *or* money market instruments, depending on market conditions. These funds give the money managers the greatest flexibility in anticipating or responding to economic changes.

Ginnie Mae or GNMA Funds seek a high level of income by investing in mortgage securities backed by the Government National Mortgage Association (GNMA). To qualify for this category, the majority of the portfolio must always be invested in mortgage-backed securities.

[1] Exception: The definition of *stock index funds* is the author's.

Global Bond Funds seek a high level of income by investing in the debt securities of companies and countries worldwide, including the United States.

Global Equity Funds seek growth in the value of their investments by investing in securities traded worldwide, including the United States. Compared to direct investments, global funds offer investors an easier avenue to investing abroad. The funds' professional money managers handle the trading and recordkeeping details and deal with differences in currencies, languages, time zones, laws and regulations, and business customs and practices. In addition to another layer of diversification, global funds add another layer of risk — exchange-rate risk.

Growth and Income Funds invest mainly in the common stock of companies that have had increasing share value but also a solid record of paying dividends. This type of fund attempts to combine long-term capital growth with a steady stream of income.

Growth Funds invest in the common stock of well-established companies. Their primary aim is to produce an increase in the value of their investments (capital gains) rather than a flow of dividends. Investors who buy a growth fund are more interested in seeing the fund's share price rise than in receiving income from dividends.

High-Yield Bond Funds maintain at least two-thirds of their portfolios in lower-rated corporate bonds (Baa or lower by Moody's rating service and BBB or lower by Standard & Poor's rating service). In return for a generally higher yield, investors must bear a greater degree of risk than for higher-rated bonds.

Income-Bond Funds seek a high level of current income by investing at all times in a mix of corporate and government bonds.

Income-Equity Funds seek a high level of current income by investing primarily in equity security of companies with good dividend-paying records.

Income-Mixed Funds seek a high level of current income by investing in income-producing securities, including both equities and debt instruments.

International Funds seek growth in the value of their investments by investing in equity securities of companies located outside the United States. Two-thirds of their portfolios must be so invested at all times to be categorized here.

Money Market Mutual Funds seek to maintain a stable net asset value by investing in the short-term, high-grade securities sold in the money market. These are generally the safest, most stable securities available and include Treasury bills, certificates of deposit of large banks, and commercial paper (the short-term IOUs of large U.S. corporations). Money market funds limit the average maturity of their portfolio to 90 days or less.

Precious Metals/Gold Funds seek an increase in the value of their investments by investing at least two-thirds of their portfolios in securities associated with gold, silver, and other precious metals.

Stock Index Funds are unmanaged funds that attempt to match the performance of an index. For example, an S&P Index fund attempts to match the S&P 500 Index.

U.S. Government Income Funds seek current income by investing in a variety of government securities, including U.S. Treasury bonds, federally guaranteed mortgage-backed securities, and other government notes.

Appendix A: Holly's Tables

References to the following tables and definitions of terms can be found in Chapter 2. As with any illustration of complex tax-advantaged instruments, there are limitations to these tables. First, a constant rate of return is assumed. In reality, the return will fluctuate, as discussed in Chapters 6 and 7, and as illustrated in two of the tables showing one holding period ending in a down market (1934–74) (Table 2) and one holding period ending in an up market (1955–95) (Table 3). In addition, all of the return is assumed to be taxed in the regular account; actual experience would result in taxation of those portions of the return attributable to dividends, interest, and capital gains. Finally, the cost of investment to the regular account is not adjusted to show what you would have had to earn in order to invest that amount after paying income taxes on those earnings. This concept is illustrated in the text in Chapter 2 (pages 31–34). Had taxes on earnings been included, the "cost of investment" for the regular account would have been higher in the tables.

The tables show different assumptions for age, employee pretax contributions, matches, and tax rates. The numbers in the tables are provided solely to illustrate how a 401(k) might differ from a regular account. They are not meant to be definitive in terms of actual experience, which will depend on taxes and returns. **In order to determine what your experience might be in your 401(k), please consult your tax and investment advisers.**

TABLE 1

Starting Age	21			
Starting Compensation	$12,000			
			Pretax Contribution	You Invested (Cost of Investment)
Pretax Contribution	4%	$480	Per Day $1.32	Per Day $1.00

	Before 65	After 65	
Rate of Return	11%	6%	Assumed to Be Tax-Free Investment After Age 65 in
Effective Tax Rate	25%	38%	Regular Account
Company Match	50%	0%	
Salary Increases	3%	0%	

	401(k)	Regular Account
By Age 65		
Pretax Contribution to 401(k)		
Comparable Investment to Regular Account	$42,000	$42,000
Out-of-Pocket Cost of Investment		
Showing Effect of Leveraged Paycheck*	$32,000	$42,000
Value of Account at Age 65		
Showing Effect of Remaining Compounding Elements	$1,000,000	$215,000
Benefit of Investing in Your 401(k) Over Your Regular Account	$785,000	
By Age 70½		
Out-of-Pocket Cost of Investment	$32,000	$42,000
Value of Account at Age 70½	$1,400,000	$325,000
Benefit of Investing in Your 401(k) Over Your Regular Account	$1,075,000	
Annual "Pension Check" You Pay Yourself (After Income Taxes)**		
At Age 71	$57,000	$19,500
At Age 81	$73,000	$19,500
At Age 91	$47,000	$19,500
Value of Account at Age 91	$300,000	$325,000

* Leveraged Paycheck lowers the cost of the 401(k) by $10,000
** Your Preretirement Paycheck (Age 65) $42,000

See Chapter 2 for definitions. These numbers are presented for illustration purposes only and will vary based on tax and performance assumptions.

TABLE 2

Starting Age	25				
Starting Compensation	$26,000				
			Pretax Contribution	**You Invested (Cost of Investment)**	
Pretax Contribution	5%	$1,300	Per Day $3.56	Per Day	$2.67
	Before 65	**After 65**			
Rate of Return	S&P	6%	Assumed to Be Tax-Free Investment After Age 65 in		
Effective Tax Rate	25%	38%	Regular Account		
Company Match	50%	0%	S&P Actual Experience Ending in a Down Market		
Salary Increases	3%	0%	(1934–74)		

	401(k)	Regular Account
By Age 65		
Pretax Contribution to 401(k)		
Comparable Investment to Regular Account	$100,000	$100,000
Out-of-Pocket Cost of Investment		
Showing Effect of Leveraged Paycheck*	$75,000	$100,000
Value of Account at Age 65		
Showing Effect of Remaining Compounding Elements	$1,000,000	$300,000
Benefit of Investing in Your 401(k) Over Your Regular Account	$700,000	
By Age 70½		
Out-of-Pocket Cost of Investment	$75,000	$100,000
Value of Account at Age 70½	$1,500,000	$400,000
Benefit of Investing in Your 401(k) Over Your Regular Account	$1,100,000	
Annual "Pension Check" You Pay Yourself (After Income Taxes)**		
At Age 71	$60,000	$24,000
At Age 81	$75,000	$24,000
At Age 91	$50,000	$24,000
Value of Account at Age 91	$320,000	$400,000

* Leveraged Paycheck lowers the cost of the 401(k) by $25,000
** Your Preretirement Paycheck (Age 65) $82,000

See Chapter 2 for definitions. These numbers are presented for illustration purposes only and will vary based on tax and performance assumptions.

TABLE 3

Starting Age	25				
Starting Compensation	$26,000				
			Pretax Contribution	You Invested (Cost of Investment)	
Pretax Contribution	5%	$1,300	Per Day $3.56	Per Day	$2.67
	Before 65	After 65			
Rate of Return	S&P	6%	Assumed to Be Tax-Free Investment After Age 65 in		
Effective Tax Rate	25%	38%	Regular Account		
Company Match	50%	0%	S&P Actual Experience Ending in an Up Market		
Salary Increases	3%	0%	(1955–95)		

	401(k)	Regular Account
By Age 65		
Pretax Contribution to 401(k)		
Comparable Investment to Regular Account	$100,000	$100,000
Out-of-Pocket Cost of Investment		
Showing Effect of Leveraged Paycheck*	$75,000	$100,000
Value of Account at Age 65		
Showing Effect of Remaining Compounding Elements	$1,850,000	$450,000
Benefit of Investing in Your 401(k) Over Your Regular Account	$1,400,000	
By Age 70½		
Out-of-Pocket Cost of Investment	$75,000	$100,000
Value of Account at Age 70½	$2,600,000	$600,000
Benefit of Investing in Your 401(k) Over Your Regular Account	$2,000,000	
Annual "Pension Check" You Pay Yourself (After Income Taxes)**		
At Age 71	$100,000	$38,100
At Age 81	$135,000	$38,100
At Age 91	$90,000	$38,100
Value of Account at Age 91	$560,000	$600,000

* Leveraged Paycheck lowers the cost of the 401(k) by $25,000
** Your Preretirement Paycheck (Age 65) $82,000

See Chapter 2 for definitions. These numbers are presented for illustration purposes only and will vary based on tax and performance assumptions.

TABLE 4

Starting Age	25			
Starting Compensation	$26,000			
			Pretax Contribution	You Invested (Cost of Investment)
Pretax Contribution	5%	$1,300	Per Day $3.56	Per Day $2.67
	Before 65	After 65		
Rate of Return	10%	6%	Assumed to Be Tax-Free Investment After Age 65 in
Effective Tax Rate	25%	38%	Regular Account
Company Match	50%	0%	
Salary Increases	3%	0%	

	401(k)	Regular Account
By Age 65		
Pretax Contribution to 401(k)		
Comparable Investment to Regular Account	$100,000	$100,000
Out-of-Pocket Cost of Investment		
Showing Effect of Leveraged Paycheck*	$75,000	$100,000
Value of Account at Age 65		
Showing Effect of Remaining Compounding Elements	$1,280,000	$345,000
Benefit of Investing in Your 401(k) Over Your Regular Account	$935,000	
By Age 70½		
Out-of-Pocket Cost of Investment	$75,000	$100,000
Value of Account at Age 70½	$1,900,000	$500,000
Benefit of Investing in Your 401(k) Over Your Regular Account	$1,400,000	
Annual "Pension Check" You Pay Yourself (After Income Taxes)**		
At Age 71	$75,000	$30,000
At Age 81	$100,000	$30,000
At Age 91	$65,000	$30,000
Value of Account at Age 91	$400,000	$500,000

* Leveraged Paycheck lowers the cost of the 401(k) by	$25,000
** Your Preretirement Paycheck (Age 65)	$82,000

See Chapter 2 for definitions. These numbers are presented for illustration purposes only and will vary based on tax and performance assumptions.

TABLE 5

Starting Age	25			
Starting Compensation	$26,000			
			Pretax Contribution	You Invested (Cost of Investment)
Pretax Contribution	1%	$260	Per Day $0.71	Per Day $0.53

	Before 65	After 65	
Rate of Return	10%	6%	Assumed to Be Tax-Free Investment After Age 65 in
Effective Tax Rate	25%	40%	Regular Account
Company Match	100%	0%	
Salary Increases	3%	0%	

	401(k)	Regular Account
By Age 65		
Pretax Contribution to 401(k)		
Comparable Investment to Regular Account	$20,000	$20,000
Out-of-Pocket Cost of Investment		
Showing Effect of Leveraged Paycheck*	$15,000	$20,000
Value of Account at Age 65		
Showing Effect of Remaining Compounding Elements	$340,000	$70,000
Benefit of Investing in Your 401(k) Over Your Regular Account	$270,000	
By Age 70½		
Out-of-Pocket Cost of Investment	$15,000	$20,000
Value of Account at Age 70½	$500,000	$100,000
Benefit of Investing in Your 401(k) Over Your Regular Account	$400,000	
Annual "Pension Check" You Pay Yourself (After Income Taxes)**		
At Age 71	$20,000	$6,000
At Age 81	$25,000	$6,000
At Age 91	$16,000	$6,000
Value of Account at Age 91	$105,000	$100,000

* Leveraged Paycheck lowers the cost of the 401(k) by	$5,000
** Your Preretirement Paycheck (Age 65)	$82,000

See Chapter 2 for definitions. These numbers are presented for illustration purposes only and will vary based on tax and performance assumptions.

TABLE 6

Starting Age	35				
Starting Compensation	$40,000				
			Pretax Contribution	You Invested (Cost of Investment)	
Pretax Contribution	6%	$2,400	Per Day $6.58	Per Day $4.93	

	Before 65	After 65	
Rate of Return	10%	6%	Assumed to Be Tax-Free Investment After Age 65 in
Effective Tax Rate	25%	40%	Regular Account
Company Match	50%	0%	
Salary Increases	3%	0%	

	401(k)	Regular Account
By Age 65		
Pretax Contribution to 401(k)		
Comparable Investment to Regular Account	$115,000	$115,000
Out-of-Pocket Cost of Investment		
Showing Effect of Leveraged Paycheck*	$86,250	$115,000
Value of Account at Age 65		
Showing Effect of Remaining Compounding Elements	$850,000	$270,000
Benefit of Investing in Your 401(k) Over Your Regular Account	$580,000	
By Age 70½		
Out-of-Pocket Cost of Investment	$86,250	$115,000
Value of Account at Age 70½	$1,250,000	$400,000
Benefit of Investing in Your 401(k) Over Your Regular Account	$850,000	
Annual "Pension Check" You Pay Yourself (After Income Taxes)**		
At Age 71	$50,000	$24,000
At Age 81	$60,000	$24,000
At Age 91	$40,000	$24,000
Value of Account at Age 91	$270,000	$400,000

* Leveraged Paycheck lowers the cost of the 401(k) by $28,750
** Your Preretirement Paycheck (Age 65) $94,000

See Chapter 2 for definitions. These numbers are presented for illustration purposes only and will vary based on tax and performance assumptions.

TABLE 7

Starting Age	45				
Starting Compensation	$50,000				
			Pretax Contribution	You Invested (Cost of Investment)	
Pretax Contribution	3%	$1,500	Per Day $4.11	Per Day	$3.08

	Before 65	After 65	
Rate of Return	10%	6%	Assumed to Be Tax-Free Investment After Age 65 in
Effective Tax Rate	25%	40%	Regular Account
Company Match	25%	0%	
Salary Increases	3%	0%	

	401(k)	Regular Account
By Age 65		
Pretax Contribution to 401(k)		
Comparable Investment to Regular Account	$40,000	$40,000
Out-of-Pocket Cost of Investment		
Showing Effect of Leveraged Paycheck*	$30,000	$40,000
Value of Account at Age 65		
Showing Effect of Remaining Compounding Elements	$145,000	$65,000
Benefit of Investing in Your 401(k) Over Your Regular Account	$80,000	
By Age 70½		
Out-of-Pocket Cost of Investment	$30,000	$40,000
Value of Account at Age 70½	$220,000	$100,000
Benefit of Investing in Your 401(k) Over Your Regular Account	$120,000	
Annual "Pension Check" You Pay Yourself (After Income Taxes)**		
At Age 71	$8,000	$6,000
At Age 81	$11,000	$6,000
At Age 91	$7,000	$6,000
Value of Account at Age 91	$46,000	$100,000

* Leveraged Paycheck lowers the cost of the 401(k) by	$10,000
** Your Preretirement Paycheck (Age 65)	$88,000

See Chapter 2 for definitions. These numbers are presented for illustration purposes only and will vary based on tax and performance assumptions.

TABLE 8

Starting Age	55				
Starting Compensation	$60,000				
			Pretax Contribution	You Invested (Cost of Investment)	
Pretax Contribution	6%	$3,600	Per Day $9.86	Per Day	$7.40

	Before 65	After 65	
Rate of Return	10%	6%	Assumed to Be Tax-Free Investment After Age 65 in
Effective Tax Rate	25%	40%	Regular Account
Company Match	25%	0%	
Salary Increases	3%	0%	

	401(k)	Regular Account
By Age 65		
Pretax Contribution to 401(k)		
Comparable Investment to Regular Account	$41,000	$41,000
Out-of-Pocket Cost of Investment		
Showing Effect of Leveraged Paycheck*	$31,000	$41,000
Value of Account at Age 65		
Showing Effect of Remaining Compounding Elements	$88,000	$46,000
Benefit of Investing in Your 401(k) Over Your Regular Account	$42,000	
By Age 70½		
Out-of-Pocket Cost of Investment	$31,000	$41,000
Value of Account at Age 70½	$140,000	$70,000
Benefit of Investing in Your 401(k) Over Your Regular Account	$70,000	
Annual "Pension Check" You Pay Yourself (After Income Taxes)**		
At Age 71	$5,500	$4,200
At Age 81	$7,000	$4,200
At Age 91	$4,500	$4,200
Value of Account at Age 91	$30,000	$70,000

* Leveraged Paycheck lowers the cost of the 401(k) by $10,000
** Your Preretirement Paycheck (Age 65) $80,000

See Chapter 2 for definitions. These numbers are presented for illustration purposes only and will vary based on tax and performance assumptions.

TABLE 9

Starting Age	60				
Starting Compensation	$60,000				
			Pretax Contribution	You Invested (Cost of Investment)	
Pretax Contribution	6%	$3,600	Per Day $9.86	Per Day	$6.41

	Before 65	After 65	
Rate of Return	6%	6%	Assumed to Be Tax-Free Investment After Age 65 in
Effective Tax Rate	35%	25%	Regular Account
Company Match	25%	0%	
Salary Increases	3%	0%	

	401(k)	Regular Account
By Age 65		
Pretax Contribution to 401(k)		
Comparable Investment to Regular Account	$20,000	$20,000
Out-of-Pocket Cost of Investment		
Showing Effect of Leveraged Paycheck*	$13,000	$20,000
Value of Account at Age 65		
Showing Effect of Remaining Compounding Elements	$28,000	$14,000
Benefit of Investing in Your 401(k) Over Your Regular Account	$14,000	
By Age 70½		
Out-of-Pocket Cost of Investment	$13,000	$20,000
Value of Account at Age 70½	$47,000	$21,000
Benefit of Investing in Your 401(k) Over Your Regular Account	$26,000	
Annual "Pension Check" You Pay Yourself (After Income Taxes)**		
At Age 71	$2,300	$1,260
At Age 81	$3,000	$1,260
At Age 91	$2,000	$1,260
Value of Account at Age 91	$10,000	$21,000

* Leveraged Paycheck lowers the cost of the 401(k) by	$7,000
** Your Preretirement Paycheck (Age 65)	$67,500

See Chapter 2 for definitions. These numbers are presented for illustration purposes only and will vary based on tax and performance assumptions.

Appendix B

Enrollment Form

THE XYZ GROUP

NAME: John Doe   SOC. SEC. #: 999-99-9999   AGE 40/$70M

CONTRIBUTION SELECTION

Based on a weekly payroll

Check one box:

	12%	10%	8%	7%	6%	5%	4%	3%	2%
1. Percent to Contribute	☐	☐	☐	☐	☐	☐	☐	☐	☐
2. Amount That Your Take-Home Paycheck Will Be Reduced	102.77	85.65	68.51	59.95	51.38	42.82	34.26	25.69	17.13
3. Estimated Tax Savings	58.77	48.97	39.18	34.28	29.39	24.49	19.59	14.69	9.79
4. Estimated Company Match	80.77	80.77	80.77	80.77	80.77	67.31	53.85	40.38	26.92
5. Total Going into Plan	242.31	215.39	188.46	175.00	161.54	134.62	107.70	80.76	53.84
6. Benefit by Participation	139.54	129.74	119.95	115.05	110.16	91.80	73.44	55.07	36.71

2 INVESTMENT ELECTION

1. ____ Money Market Fund
2. ____ Bond Fund
3. ____ Balanced Account
4. ____ Common Stock Account
5. ____ Aggressive Stock Fund

         100% Total

Source: BISYS Plan Services of Ambler, PA, and The American Funds Group

184

3 PROJECTED BENEFITS

Based on 4% contribution to the plan:

Projected Benefits at Age 65:

If you start today	$703,925
If you wait 5 years	$427,114
Cost of waiting	$276,811

Based on 6% contribution to the plan:

Projected Benefits at Age 65:

If you start today	$1,055,827
If you wait 5 years	$ 640,635
Cost of waiting	$ 415,192

This is only an example and not intended as a projection or guarantee. It is based on company records of age and salary and assumes a 9 percent overall rate of return on investment. Your actual results will be different and are based only on how much you contribute and how your investments actually perform over time.

185

STATEMENT OF ACCOUNT
(PLAN SUMMARY)

John Doe
Social Security Number: 999-99-9999

	01/01/XX BALANCE	CONTRIBUTIONS	LOAN REPAYMENTS	INVESTMENT EARNINGS	03/31/XX BALANCE	VESTED BALANCE
EMPLOYEE 401(K)						
EuroPacific Growth Fund	10407.98	104.34	.00	1142.38	11654.70	11654.70
The New Economy Fund	756.37	104.31	.00	62.66	923.34	923.34
American Balanced Fund	450.16	104.32	.00	(32.68)	521.80	521.80
Intermediate Bond Fund	604.36	104.33	.00	11.82	720.51	720.51
Cash Management Trust						
EMPLOYER MATCH						
EuroPacifc Growth Fund	2964.16	46.14	.00	325.30	3335.60	1334.24
The New Economy Fund	198.16	46.16	.00	16.82	261.14	104.46
American Balanced Fund	117.87	46.14	.00	(16.69)	147.32	58.92
Intermediate Bond Fund	153.44	46.14	.00	3.46	203.04	81.21
Cash Management Trust						

Source: BISYS Plan Services of Ambler, PA, and The American Funds Group.

EMPLOYER PROFIT SHARING

EuroPacific Growth Fund	3390.21	196.12	.00	386.66	3972.99	1589.20
The New Economy Fund	77.08	196.12	.00	16.18	289.38	115.74
American Balanced Fund	46.02	196.12	.00	(80.53)	161.61	64.65
Intermediate Bond Fund	21.75	196.12	.00	4.66	222.53	89.01
Cash Management Trust						

TOTAL ACCOUNTS

EuroPacific Growth Fund	16762.35	346.60	.00	1854.34	18963.29	14578.14
The New Economy Fund	1031.61	346.59	.00	95.66	1473.86	1143.54
American Balanced Fund	614.05	346.58	.00	(129.90)	830.73	645.37
Intermediate Bond Fund	779.55	346.59	.00	19.94	1146.08	890.73
Cash Management Trust						

GRAND TOTAL	19187.56	1386.36	.00	1840.04	22413.96	17257.78

Your Investment Mix as of 03/31/XX

EuroPacific Growth Fund	85% of Assets
The New Economy Fund	6% of Assets
American Balanced Fund	4% of Assets
Intermediate Bond Fund	5% of Assets
Cash Management Trust	0% of Assets

STATEMENT OF ACCOUNT
(TRANSACTION DETAILS)

EUROPACIFIC GROWTH FUND

DATE	TYPE OF TRANSACTION	DOLLARS	SHARE PRICE	SHARES PURCH/SOLD	TOTAL SHARES HELD	TOTAL DOLLAR VALUE
12/31/XX	Beg. Balance		18.20		921.007	16762.33
01/09/XX	Dividend	0.67	18.36	.036	921.043	16910.35
01/09/XX	STIF*	0.02	18.36	.001	921.044	16910.37
01/29/XX	Payroll Cont.	226.22	18.73	12.078	933.122	17477.38
02/13/XX	Dividend	1.10	19.44	.057	933.179	18141.00
02/20/XX	Payroll Cont.	60.19	19.94	3.019	936.198	18667.79
02/25/XX	STIF	0.17	19.81	.009	936.207	18546.26
03/10/XX	Dividend	1.04	20.38	.051	936.258	19080.94
03/20/XX	Payroll Cont.	60.19	20.19	2.982	939.240	18963.26
03/24/XX	STIF	0.04	20.05	.001	939.241	18831.78
03/31/XX	End. Balance		20.19		939.241	18963.28

* Short-Term Interest Fund

STATEMENT OF ACCOUNT
(TRANSACTION DETAILS)

THE NEW ECONOMY FUND

DATE	TYPE OF TRANSACTION	DOLLARS	SHARE PRICE	SHARES PURCH/SOLD	TOTAL SHARES HELD	TOTAL DOLLAR VALUE
12/31/XX	Beg. Balance		29.82		34.594	1031.59
01/09/XX	STIF*	0.02	30.05	.001	34.595	1039.58
01/29/XX	Payroll Cont.	226.21	30.60	7.393	41.988	1284.83
02/20/XX	Payroll Cont.	60.19	31.20	1.929	43.917	1370.21
02/25/XX	STIF	0.17	31.51	.005	43.922	1383.98
03/20/XX	Payroll Cont.	60.19	31.60	1.905	45.827	1448.13
03/24/XX	STIF	0.04	31.92	.001	45.828	1462.83
03/31/XX	End. Balance		32.16		45.828	1473.83

* Short-Term Interest Fund

STATEMENT OF ACCOUNT
(TRANSACTION DETAILS)

AMERICAN BALANCED FUND

DATE	TYPE OF TRANSACTION	DOLLARS	SHARE PRICE	SHARES PURCH/SOLD	TOTAL SHARES HELD	TOTAL DOLLAR VALUE
12/31/XX	Beg. Balance		12.78		48.046	614.03
01/09/XX	STIF*	0.02	12.79	.002	48.048	614.53
01/29/XX	Payroll Cont.	226.22	12.87	17.578	65.626	844.61
01/31/XX	Dividend	3.42	12.83	.267	65.893	845.41
02/20/XX	Payroll Cont.	60.18	12.95	4.647	70.540	913.49
02/25/XX	STIF	0.17	13.03	.014	70.554	919.32
02/27/XX	Dividend	3.83	13.05	.293	70.847	924.55
03/20/XX	Payroll Cont.	60.18	12.99	4.633	75.480	980.49
03/24/XX	Dividend	4.19	13.02	.322	75.802	986.94
03/24/XX	STIF	0.04	13.02	.003	75.805	986.98
03/31/XX	End. Balance		13.01		75.805	986.22

* Short-Term Interest Fund

STATEMENT OF ACCOUNT
(TRANSACTION DETAILS)

INTERMEDIATE BOND FUND

DATE	TYPE OF TRANSACTION	DOLLARS	SHARE PRICE	SHARES PURCH/SOLD	TOTAL SHARES HELD	TOTAL DOLLAR VALUE
12/31/XX	Beg. Balance		14.53		53.650	779.53
01/09/XX	STIF*	0.02	14.54	.001	53.651	780.09
01/29/XX	Payroll Cont.	226.21	14.51	15.590	69.241	1004.69
01/31/XX	Dividend	3.99	14.49	.275	69.516	1007.29
02/20/XX	Payroll Cont.	60.19	14.57	4.131	73.647	1073.04
02/25/XX	STIF	0.17	14.62	.012	73.659	1076.89
02/27/XX	Dividend	4.32	14.63	.295	73.954	1081.95
02/28/XX	Dividend	1.19	14.65	.081	74.035	1084.61
03/20/XX	Payroll Cont.	60.19	14.63	4.114	78.149	1143.32
03/24/XX	Dividend	4.65	14.62	.318	78.467	1147.19
03/24/XX	STIF	0.04	14.62	.003	78.470	1147.23
03/31/XX	End. Balance		14.62		78.470	1147.23

* Short-Term Interest Fund

STATEMENT OF ACCOUNT
(TRANSACTION DETAILS)

CASH MANAGEMENT TRUST

DATE	TYPE OF TRANSACTION	DOLLARS	SHARE PRICE	SHARES PURCH/SOLD	TOTAL SHARES HELD	TOTAL DOLLAR VALUE
12/31/XX	Beg. Balance		1.00		.000	0.00
03/31/XX	End. Balance		1.00		.000	0.00

Appendix C

HIGHLY COMPENSATED TABLE 1996 LIMITS

Salary $240,000
Maximum Legal Limit: $150,000
Employee's Voluntary Contribution: 9%
Match: 66⅔% on Pretax Only, up to 6% of Salary

		TEST #1 ELECTIVE DEFERRAL LIMIT						TEST #2 SECTION 415 LIMITS						
	EMPLOYEE CONTRIBUTION	ANNUAL CAP $9,500	ROOM LEFT	PRETAX	CUMULATIVE PRETAX	AFTER-TAX	CUMULATIVE AFTER-TAX	ANNUAL CAP IS LESSER OF 25.00%	$30,000	$30,000	CUMULATIVE CONTRIBUTION	MATCH	PLAN TOTAL	CUMULATIVE PLAN TOTAL	415 ROOM LEFT
JAN	$1,125*	$9,500	$8,375	$1,125	$1,125	$0	$0	$37,500	$30,000	$30,000	$1,125	$750	$1,875	$1,875	$28,125
FEB	$1,125	$9,500	$7,250	$1,125	$2,250	$0	$0	N/A	$30,000	$30,000	$2,250	$750	$1,875	$3,750	$26,250
MAR	$1,125	$9,500	$6,125	$1,125	$3,375	$0	$0	N/A	$30,000	$30,000	$3,375	$750	$1,875	$5,625	$24,375
APR	$1,125	$9,500	$5,000	$1,125	$4,500	$0	$0	N/A	$30,000	$30,000	$4,500	$750	$1,875	$7,500	$22,500
MAY	$1,125	$9,500	$3,875	$1,125	$5,625	$0	$0	N/A	$30,000	$30,000	$5,625	$750	$1,875	$9,375	$20,625
JUN	$1,125	$9,500	$2,750	$1,125	$6,750	$0	$0	N/A	$30,000	$30,000	$6,750	$750	$1,875	$11,250	$18,750
JUL	$1,125	$9,500	$1,625	$1,125	$7,875	$0	$0	N/A	$30,000	$30,000	$7,875	$750	$1,875	$13,124	$16,876
AUG	$1,125	$9,500	$500	$1,125	$9,000	$0	$0	N/A	$30,000	$30,000	$9,000	$750	$1,875	$14,999	$15,001
SEP	$1,125	$9,500	$0	$500	$9,500	$625	$625	N/A	$30,000	$30,000	$10,125	$333	$1,458	$16,458	$13,542
OCT	$1,125	$9,500	$0	$0	$9,500	$1,125	$1,125	N/A	$30,000	$30,000	$11,250	$0	$1,125	$17,583	$12,417
NOV	$1,125	$9,500	$0	$0	$9,500	$1,125	$1,125	N/A	$30,000	$30,000	$12,375	$0	$1,125	$18,708	$11,292
DEC	$1,125	$9,500	$0	$0	$9,500	$1,125	$1,125	N/A	$30,000	$30,000	$13,500	$0	$1,125	$19,833	$10,167
	$13,500			$9,500		$4,000						$6,333	$19,833		

* ($150,000 ÷ 12) × 9% = $1,125

194

Index

75, 140–42, 146, 149, 152–53,
156, 172, 173–81
questionnaire on, 66, 75–76, 77
rate of, 156
retirement income and, 82, 128–32
strategy for, 68–74
taxation and, 68–69, 76, 77
tests for maximum, 152–53
corporate bond funds, 30, 167
corporate bonds, 30, 167, 168
cost of living adjustments, 20–21, 128
court orders, 151
creditors, 151
credit risk, 14, 82, 84–85, 88–89
cumulative return, 145
currency exchange risk, 83n, 168

death, 15, 49, 50, 55, 58, 141, 154
decision-making, 61–65, 77, 82, 156
defaults, loan, 146, 151–52
Depression, Great, 105, 106
"Directory of Mutual Funds," 154
disability, 15, 49, 55, 58, 140, 141, 148, 154, 158
disclosure statements, 154
"discrimination testing," 50
diversification, 84, 85, 88–89, 111, 117, 119, 160
dividends, 18, 25, 37, 38, 96, 114, 115, 126, 144, 145, 168, 171
divorce, 140, 151
dollar benefit, 70–71
Dow Jones Industrial Average, 84–85

effective tax rate, calculating, 43
elective contributions, 48, 58
elective deferral limit, 152, 153
Employee Retirement Income
Security Act of 1974 (ERISA), 54, 155

enhancement techniques, 14, 163
enrollment forms, 49, 110, 140, 143, 184–85
equity, 118, 168, 169
estate taxes, 132, 140, 149–50, 158, 161
excess taxes, 129, 150

Federal Insurance Contributions Act (FICA), 29, 134n
fiduciaries, 155–56
financial hardship, 15, 48, 54, 58, 141, 154, 157
financial reports, 160
five-year averaging, 142, 149
fixed income funds, 114–15, 124
flexible portfolio funds, 167
forfeitures, 59, 144, 154
Franklin AGE High Income Fund, 119, 120
401(k) plan:
account statements for, 140, 144–45, 186–92
administrators of, 49, 74, 154, 155–56, 158–59
advantages of, 23–46
after-tax contributions to, 19, 24, 37, 40, 48, 51, 52, 54, 56, 57, 58, 59, 60, 67, 69, 75, 140–41, 142, 149, 152, 153, 156
asset base for, 23, 64, 86, 88, 93, 105, 110–11, 112, 117, 159, 165
beneficiaries of, 142, 149–51, 154, 158, 159
bonuses for, 18, 24, 25, 41, 52, 63, 69, 71, 72, 135
budgets and, 13, 63, 66, 73–74, 77, 133–34
calendars for, 156
common mistakes on, 133–39
as company "savings" plan, 20, 68–69

About the Author

Julie Jason, JD, LLM, has been involved in the securities industry since graduating from law school in 1975, first as a lawyer and later as a manager and investment adviser. She is Managing Director of Jackson, Grant & Company and Jackson, Grant Investment Advisers, Inc., registered broker/dealers and investment advisers, respectively, of Stamford, Connecticut. Ms. Jason manages money for individual investors. A frequent lecturer, Ms. Jason teaches investment principles in educational programs for 401(k) participants and in continuing education programs for attorneys, accountants, and the general public. Ms. Jason is the author of an upcoming book for 401(k) plan sponsors to be published by Prentice-Hall, which guides employers through the process of setting up and managing a 401(k) plan for their employees. Jackson, Grant & Company is located in Stamford, CT.